DEATH, THE DEAD AND POPULAR CULTURE

BY

RUTH PENFOLD-MOUNCE
University of York, UK

emerald
PUBLISHING

United Kingdom – North America – Japan – India
Malaysia – China

Emerald Publishing Limited
Howard House, Wagon Lane, Bingley BD16 1WA, UK

First edition 2018

Reprints and permissions service
Contact: permissions@emeraldinsight.com

British Library Cataloguing in Publication Data
A catalogue record for this book is available from the British
Library

ISBN: 978-1-78743-054-9 (paperback)
ISBN: 978-1-78743-053-2 (E-ISBN)
ISBN: 978-1-78743-943-6 (Epub)

Printed and bound by CPI Group (UK) Ltd, Croydon, CR0 4YY

ISOQAR certified
Management System,
awarded to Emerald
for adherence to
Environmental
standard
ISO 14001:2004.

ISOQAR
REGISTERED
Certificate Number 1985
ISO 14001

INVESTOR IN PEOPLE

UNIVERSITY OF
WINCHESTER

Martial Rose Library
Tel: 01962 827306

EMERALD STUDIES IN DEATH AND CULTURE

Series Editors:
Ruth Penfold-Mounce, University of York, UK
Julie Rugg, University of York, UK
Jack Denham, York St John University, UK

Editorial Advisory Board: Jacque Lynn Foltyn, National University, USA; Lisa McCormick, University of Edinburgh, UK; Ben Poore, University of York, UK; Melissa Schrift, East Tennessee State University, USA; Kate Woodthorpe, University of Bath, UK

Emerald Studies in Death and Culture provides an outlet for cross-disciplinary exploration of aspects of mortality. The series creates a new forum for the publication of interdisciplinary research that approaches death from a cultural perspective. Published texts will be at the forefront of new ideas, new subjects, new theoretical applications, and new explorations of less conventional cultural engagements with death and the dead.

Published Titles

Brian Parsons, *The Evolution of the British Funeral Industry in the 20th Century: From Undertaker to Funeral Director*

Forthcoming Titles

Tim Bullamore, *The Art of Obituary Writing*

Matthew Spokes, Jack Denham, and Benedikt Lehmann, *Death, Memorialization and Deviant Spaces*

Racheal Harris, *Meaning and Symbolism in Pet Inspired Memorial Tattoos: Echoes and Imitations of Life*

CONTENTS

LIST OF FIGURES

PREFACE

My fascination with death and the dead goes back to my doctoral studies (2001–2005) when I came across tales of doctors keeping body parts taken from famous dead criminals whom they had autopsied. Combining this macabre souvenir trade in the dead with popular culture was a remarkably easy step considering my wider interest in celebrity and popular culture. I have come to embrace the quote by JM Barrie's well-loved character Peter Pan (Peter Pan, 1911) who said that to die would be an awfully big adventure. Pan got it almost right but failed to mention that to research death is a big adventure, too, and this book is proof of that.

Death, The Dead and Popular Culture is part of the first wave of publications under the Emerald Series in Death and Culture which was inspired by the first biennial Death and Culture Conference held at the University of York, UK, in 2016. The book series is driven by the intention of providing an outlet for cross-disciplinary exploration of aspects of mortality. It seeks to provide a forum for research that approaches death from a cultural perspective and is fully supportive of new ideas and subjects, new theoretical applications, and new explorations of less conventional engagements with death and the dead. The *Emerald Series in Death and Culture* is run by myself, Dr Julie Rugg (University of York, UK), and Dr Jack Denham (York St John University, UK), and we put out a call for book proposals in January 2017. So far, in these early stages, we have been successful to recruit passionate researchers working in fascinating fields of death research and we look forward to publishing many books in the future.

My contribution to death studies research extends beyond the book series and conference and has branched out to include the establishment of the Death and Culture Network (DaCNet) at the University of York, UK. This interdisciplinary network brings together scholars with an interest in death, provides support and training for doctoral researchers rooted in death studies, and actively pursues public engagement. The hope for DaCNet in the future is to provide leadership and a sense of unity to the international community of death scholars who examine the vibrant and diverse relationship between death and culture in all its varied forms.

Much gratitude goes to Philippa Grand and Emerald Publishing for not just being willing to publish this book but to support the Emerald Series on Death and Culture.

I presented versions of chapter two at the Centre for Death and Society Conference (CDAS) in 2016 and as a Keynote Speaker at Death and the Maiden Conference in Lodz, Poland, in 2017. Both of these conferences were crucial in refining my ideas, so thank you CDAS and Kasia Malecka for persuading me to renew my passport and visit her fabulous homeland.

Thanks are also due to Dave Beer for his support, endless encouragement and much-needed lunch breaks. This book has benefitted hugely from his insight and prevented chapter three from being scrapped in its entirety in a fit of pique and self-doubt as well as rescuing chapter four with an improved framework.

My love and thanks as ever go to Daniel for good-humouredly putting up with my macabre enthusiasm for death and corpses ('There's a mummified arm in Wiltshire!') and to Abi and Sam who know far more about death and the dead than the average children under eight.

Dr Ruth Penfold-Mounce
University of York

1

INTRODUCTION: THE AGENCY OF THE DEAD

The dead are inanimate body remains and for all intents and purposes, they lack power, control, or a voice. They are a life that has ended. They have shifted from one state of being to another. But death is not that simple. The dead can, and do, have agency; in this context agency refers to a mode of action whereby the dead are considered able to influence and alter the world despite death. In 1988, Bob Dylan wrote *Death Is Not the End* and he was right. This book is not about dying or grieving, and it is not about the practicalities of death and the death industry or even rituals of death-although these are vital lines of research. Instead, this book is about how death is not the end but a beginning, albeit a posthumous one. It considers how death and the dead possess value and the ability to entertain making them into a central, commonplace phenomenon consumed by a plethora of international individuals from around the globe. Remarkably, few sociologists and even fewer death studies scholars have devoted their research energy toward an in-depth examination of the relationship among death, the dead and popular culture. This is despite popular culture being central to shaping everyday lives and practices as well as the ordering of routine experiences as part of an emerging commodified global society. Instead, scholars have chosen to focus on a wide variety of death, dying and disposal issues, including but not limited to the following: bereavement and memorialisation (Woodthorpe, 2011a); the history and policy surrounding cemetery space (Rugg, 2000; 2006; Woodthorpe, 2011b); the work of funeral directors (Howarth, 2016); consuming dark tourism sites (Stone & Sharpley, 2008; Sharpley & Stone, 2009); and even the complexity surrounding talking about death in relation to disorders of consciousness (Kitzinger & Kitzinger, 2014). In contrast to death scholarship focusing on the practicalities and industry around death, Bronfen (1992) conducted some initial work on death and its portrayal in the print media. Others also addressed death in the media but not the dead body (McIlwain, 2005; Akass & McCabe, 2005; Klaver, 2006; Kellehear, 2007). It was Foltyn, in 2008, who led the way by focusing explicitly on depictions of the dead in contemporary television shows. This was ultimately followed by a comprehensive engagement with the dead in television by Weber (2014). This book intends to rectify the gap in considering representations of death and the dead within popular culture (and not just television) and in arguing that, in a global consumer culture, corpses are gaining unprecedented agency.

As visions of the dead appear everywhere in popular culture, death and the dead are being widely consumed, demonstrating an allure that is hard to resist and stretches from literature and television to film and fashion. Death and the dead appear in stories and images from different storytelling genres, all of which embrace them at the heart of their narrative, including comedies focused on death (*Monty Python's The Meaning of Life*, 1983; *BeetleJuice*, 1988; and *Death Becomes Her*, 1992) to dramas based in the death industry

(*Six Feet Under*, 2001–2005). Even new genres have developed to represent death and the dead, such as forensic fairy tales (*Pushing Daisies*, 2007-2009) appearing alongside traditional crime television dramas (*Silent Witness*, 1996-present; *CSI: Crime Scene Investigation*, 2000–2015; and *Bones*, 2005–2017) and internationally renowned crime novels by writers such as Val McDermid, Karin Slaughter and Patricia Cornwell. Popular culture centralises the dead in the public mind. Death has acquired such prominence, particularly on television in relation to crime, that it has become a mediated public spectacle suggesting that death has arguably become 'a popular culture commodity and an acceptable form of entertainment' (Khapeava, 2017: 182). Popular culture due to its populist nature has laid the foundations for the easy appeal and consumption of death and the dead; they are ever-present and far from being denied, repressed or a societal taboo. Openly consumed images of death and corpses in multiple entertainment formats make them a banal part of everyday life that has infiltrated mass consumption.

This book engages with popular culture as the consumable mediated goods or services that ordinary people consume rather than just an educated elite. Popular culture is easily accessible, a pleasure to consume, hard to avoid in a mediated world, and a medium through which people tell and access stories. It may be an apparently frivolous and glossy topic, but popular culture has an innate value and hidden depths as a data source, especially within academic scholarship (Beer & Penfold-Mounce, 2010; Penfold-Mounce, 2015). It is where a 'creative and complex cultural conversation' creates and perpetuates rich narratives that allow an engagement with what it means to die and what it takes to matter in the world (Jones & Jensen, 2005: xxii). So, although much of popular culture is by nature 'populist', 'entertaining' and even 'fun', it provides an insight into subjects and issues traditionally considered worthy of wider academic consideration, such as class, consumption, religion, and crime (Penfold-Mounce, 2015: 257). Furthermore, by drawing on popular culture as data, it enables the researcher to tap into societal and cultural trends that cross generations, regions, and time on a mass basis. As a result, popular culture focused on death has a great deal to reveal about mass cultural perceptions and acceptance of death and the dead themselves. Importantly, it also provides a lens through which the gaze can penetrate and consume the dead and death whilst at a safe distance (Penfold-Mounce, 2015). Consequently, popular culture provides crucial and valuable insights into perceptions of mortality.

Popular culture portrayals of death grant the dead agency as a universal connection with the living. This can be taken further according to Foltyn (2008a: 103) who asserts 'the living hover around the dead, demand that they entertain them, and [try to make] the corpse into manageable, useful entities'. The dead are useful and influential through their agency and the capacity to act in a given environment even though they are deceased. This agency is exerted in diverse ways including the living enacting the dead person's wishes after death or acting on their behalf with permission from the deceased's family or through the dead's ability to stimulate a response from the individual consumer as an entity of entertainment. The active role of the dead in popular culture articulates their ability to exert influence on consumers at a symbolic, economic, or entertainment level. The dead have power over and upon the living consumer.

The pervasive ordinariness of death and the dead in popular culture highlights a normalisation of the presence of death outside personal experience or the death industry. It is not questioned but accepted and consumed. This reflects Baudrillard's now classic argument in *Symbolic Exchange and Death* (1993) that asserts capitalist society has made life and death exchangeable, rather than mutually exclusive. In this context, meaning is mortal whilst images and seduction (or consumption) of these images are immortal. This is pertinent for this book's focus on death and the dead within popular culture. For the dead are these immortal images seducing the consumer and blurring the boundary between death and life, thereby complicating understandings of mortality. This book, by focusing on popular culture, seeks to expand and unify the cacophony of voices that have debated representations of death and the dead (Foltyn, 2008b; 2011; Walter, 2009; Woodthorpe, 2010). Death and the dead occupy a prominent place in popular culture (Durkin, 2003) and, as such, are considered here to present interesting insights into understandings of death. This research will add its own distinctive and original contribution to the debate focusing on the agency of death and the dead as they are represented within a globally consumed popular culture. The concept of the dead possessing agency provides a vital arena for safely exploring cultural fears, norms, traditions, and perceptions about mortality. Popular culture will be used to emphasise that it is far from just being frivolous and superficial but is actually a central arena for 'symbolically negotiating authenticity, ownership, memory, and identity, all within the institutional processes of mass mediation' (Jones & Jenson, 2005: xvi). Consequently, popular culture is a vehicle that grants and mobilises the agency of the dead.

THE STRUCTURE AND CONTENT OF THE BOOK

The argument that the dead within popular culture have agency challenges the understanding that the dead are simply the inanimate remains of a person. It also expands death scholarship, which is dominated by research on the death

industry and the process of corpse disposal as well as grieving. Published research combining popular culture and death
is limited. There is some insightful work on death, fashion,
and celebrity by Foltyn (2008b; 2011) and most recently
a focus on the cult of death and popular culture from a
humanities perspective by Khapaeva (2017). This book seeks
to develop research that has been conducted into the representation of the dead in popular culture and asserts the
dead as possessing significant agency. This agency is evident
through the value it generates and wields amongst the living
and the multiple representations of the dead in popular culture, making them an everyday and banal form of entertainment. Death itself may mark the end of an individual, but it
creates new agency for the dead. It is this agency that lies at
the heart of this book.

In the opening analysis chapter, the symbolic and commercial
value of the dead as a form of agency will be considered through
the posthumous careers of the celebrity dead (Chapter 2).
The value of death is deliberated as a successful career move
for many well-known individuals. Being dead can rejuvenate,
reinvent, and protect the celebrities from their (often) destructive live selves and lead to a thriving celebrity career. Even
though the celebrities' physical bodies are gone, their image
survives and is perpetuated in disconcertingly vivid and lifelike ways. As such, the celebrity dead do not leave us. A range
of celebrity posthumous careers including Michael Jackson,
Elizabeth Taylor, Marilyn Monroe, and Robin Williams are
used to illuminate the agency of the dead through the symbolic and economic value they engender.

Moving on from the value and influence of dead celebrities the argument will examine the agency of the dead body
in pieces via the mythology portrayed in popular culture surrounding organ transplantation (Chapter 3). This chapter
examines the enduring Western popular culture mythology

surrounding organ transplantation and its representation within popular culture. The value of the corpse is explored through transplantation where the dead bridge death by entering another person's body and life. This posthumous second life in transplantation mythology reveals significant agency possessed by the dead via conflict between donated organ and recipient. Agency is also conveyed by organ transplantation mythology as a valuable symbolic tool that encapsulates cultural and societal beliefs about identity, control, inequality, and trust. Particular attention is paid to the crossover of myth and science through cellular memory.

Chapter 4 explores the agency wielded by popular culture representations of the reanimated corpse in the form of the Undead. The Undead (limited here to refer to zombies and vampires) are a tool through which to introduce the new concept of morbid sensibility, which illustrates how individuals and society become open to deliberating mortality within popular culture. They also expand the concept of morbid space (Penfold-Mounce, 2015) which conceptualises spaces defined by death and the dead and how these spaces are moved through, lived within, and consumed. 'Safe' and 'provocative' morbid spaces are introduced through the agency of the Undead to create a sanctuary for morbid sensibilities to be mobilised.

In Chapter 5, the focus is upon the agency of the authentic dead (fictional but realistic dead) in popular culture. The authentic dead are used to illustrate a challenge to public wisdom that contemporary Western society is in death denial and that death is taboo. By becoming anything but extraordinary, or repellent and unusual, the authentic dead annul controversy about gazing upon the dead. They form a palatable and normative bridge between viewers and the dead, particularly through channelling the gaze of the viewer through the lens of the scientific expert.

The book concludes in Chapter 6 with a sequence of reflections on encountering the agency of the dead in popular culture. An explicit version of the central arguments relating to agency is outlined along with thoughts on the original contribution made by the book to death studies and sociology scholarship through its focus on popular culture in relation to death and the dead.

The book is driven by the argument that the dead possess agency within popular culture with the intention to provoke and open further. The chapters seek to develop a sense of the intersectionality among death, the dead, and popular culture whilst suggesting various concepts as a framework to enable engagement with the relationship they share. We begin by examining the agency of the dead through the value they engender via posthumous celebrity careers.

2

POSTHUMOUS CAREERS
OF CELEBRITIES

For many famous individuals, dying is a successful and lucrative career move, and if the transition from life to death is handled carefully then well-known figures who have died can exert considerable agency leading to a thriving posthumous celebrity career. Dying can do more than simply immortalising some famous individuals. It can rejuvenate, reinvent and protect celebrities from their (often) destructive live self; death does not terminate the agency of the well-known individual. Therefore, death can be positive as it enables the survival of a celebrity image and career and creates a successful posthumous existence that wields power and influence. Dead celebrities are a route for journalists, businesses and individual consumers to engage in collective nostalgia which accords some figures, iconic popular culture status (Kitch & Hume, 2008: xx). In recent years, the demise of a celebrity means the physical body is gone but his or her image survives and is perpetuated in lifelike ways that are at times disquieting. The celebrity dead do not leave us, and they retain the ability to interact and affect individuals in society. In fact, the 'absence of the recorded star, their presence as recording, is the reason why the worship of stars is a cult of the dead' (Frow, 1998: 205–206). This chapter will use the growing number of celebrities who experience death as the beginning of a new phase of their celebrity career. These dead celebrities highlight more than the relationship between capitalism and celebrity whereby they become brands. Instead, they demonstrate the agency of the dead as a form of entrepreneurialism whereby death marks a new dimension in which to construct value through economic activity as part of a posthumous career.

The relationship between celebrity and death is explored via a focus on the value of the celebrity dead through the posthumous careers of celebrities. It seeks to contradict what actor Jonathan Rhys-Meyers stated in an interview that, 'Celebrity has lost its value—all you have to do is go on a reality TV show for six weeks and everybody knows your name.'[1] Instead, it will be argued that celebrity as a phenomenon has not lost its value, but that due to different forms and degrees of celebrity status, some celebrities simply have more value than others. Just as there are A-list and Z-list celebrities in life, so there are in death, and this chapter will focus on the former who maintain a high-profile posthumous career. Exerting influence and agency, whilst dead, and having a successful career is possible, and this chapter highlights how the celebrity dead possess both symbolic and economic value which can be maintained and increased due to their death. The intention is to go further than McCormick's (2015) work on dead classical composers and Heinich's (1996) focus on the painter Van Gogh. The intention here is not to focus on the commemoration of the 'special dead' but instead to consider dead celebrities as active products that are created, managed and finally consumed. Notably, the agency of the celebrity dead is interpreted here as their ability to continue high-profile careers after death. This is achieved in a number of ways, including performing and producing 'new' products, albeit this is due to audio and visual technologies and without explicit personal permission from the dead celebrity. Dead celebrity posthumous careers display the agency of the dead, but this is mobilised by the living who 'own' them in death.

The focus will be upon mediated celebrities rather than pre-mediated celebrities as defined in my book *Celebrity Culture and Crime* (2009) and Rojek's (2001) typology of celebrity. This embraces Giles' (2000) argument that fame and celebrity are different phenomena whereby the former is a social process and the latter is a cultural phenomenon. Celebrity is considered separate to the well-known-ness or fame achieved by those in a pre-mediated age and which has continued in a posthumous career; including, but not limited to, composers, artists, politicians and scientists. Therefore, the focus is upon 20th century celebrities onwards as this can be defined as the mediated age with the rise of mass then digital media forms. Celebrities when they die leave a distinct trace in the world through media technology that can maintain their posthumous careers indefinitely. This work seeks to take Kearl's (2010) work on post-selves further by arguing that dead celebrities are participating in an active continuation of their careers rather than a passive afterlife. The celebrity dead have agency and are subsequently thriving in their posthumous careers.

Three different but significant aspects of the symbolic and commercial value of the celebrity dead as forms of agency will be addressed in this chapter. Firstly, the celebrity dead are examined as possessing symbolic value and agency by being contemporary parables about morality and social norms. Secondly, death is explored not as an end but as a new commercially lucrative posthumous stage in a celebrity career, and thirdly, the financial implications of a posthumous career are examined particularly in regard to agency and ownership of the dead.

DEAD CELEBRITY PARABLES

In life, celebrities symbolise a widely held interpretation of success. They have talent, beauty and wealth. Celebrities are viewed as special and widely recognised making them feted around the world. As such, celebrities represent many aspirations and goals shared by individuals around the globe because the celebrities are considered desirable and live desirable lives. Consequently, the celebrities' social role is not to be lightly undertaken as they bear responsibility, according to Giles (2017: 97), to the individuals who consume them ranging from 'the governance of the self, to moral and ideological public standards'. How seriously this role is taken by many celebrities is questionable; however, what is not questionable is that celebrities do have a significant agency as they are able to influence consumers. This influence is significant as celebrities are selected and used by people to 'address and negotiate individual as well as communal, social, cultural, and political meanings' (Jensen, 2005: xvii). Influence over individuals continues after their demise for celebrities as the cause of death and their age allows them to continue their social role as symbolic guides to a global consumer market. Dead celebrities have considerable agency, therefore, in posthumous careers, particularly through their symbolic value as a contemporary parable whereby they teach a moral or spiritual lesson. The death of a celebrity can become a parable that encourages diverse global consumers to explore their shared or fragmented views on morality and social norms. As contemporary parables dead celebrities allow for

> a democratised participation in reading the present and the past in finding commonality, in exploring anonymity and fame, in connecting across time and space, race, class, and ethnicity, and [...] recognising

the constructedness of the interpretative process.
(Jensen, 2005: xxii).

Consequently, the celebrity dead are central to the affirmation of social norms, morals and values to global consumers
and become a vehicle through which disparate cultures and
peoples attain a sense of unity and a shared moral compass.
As social glue, the celebrity dead and their posthumous
careers symbolically bind individuals together. This symbolic
power is encapsulated by the global response to 2016, which
was an exceptionally productive year for adding to the ranks of
the celebrity dead. The unanticipated boom in celebrity deaths
was particularly evident (although not exclusively) in Britain
and in the United States. It marked the demise of national, international and globally renowned celebrities including but not
limited to: singer-songwriter David Bowie, actor Alan Rickman,
radio and television presenter Terry Wogan, magician Paul
Daniels, singer Merle Haggard, comedians Victoria Wood and
Ronnie Corbett, musician Prince, ventriloquist Keith Harris,
boxing legend Muhammed Ali, actor Gene Wilder, actress and
comedienne Carrie Fisher and Fisher's mother, actress Debbie
Reynolds and also singer-songwriter George Michael. The
huge influx of celebrity deaths led to 2016 being described as
an unlucky year, and Twitter was rife with discussions of each
new celebrity death with many tweets bemoaning the year that
claimed so many beloved stars. Even celebrities themselves took
to the Twittersphere including UK television presenters Ant and
Dec asking: 'Could amazing people just stop dying for a bit?
Thanks. D' (24th March 2016). There were repeated calls for
the protection of some celebrities such as legendary television
presenter and zoologist, David Attenborough:

somebody needs to find David Attenborough and
keep him safe, I don't trust 2016 anymore
(@ItsDGreenhalgh, 21st April 2016).

> David Attenborough is a National Treasure. Protect
> at all costs. He needs 24/7 security, if the man
> sneezes we need to know he's still okay (@Y2SHAF,
> 25th December 2016)

Although these tweets reflect a certain light-hearted atti-
tude towards the celebrity deaths of 2016, and though
90-year-old David Attenborough cannot really be protected
from death, the tweets do reflect an underlying unified surprise and anxiety at an apparent influx of celebrity losses. The
increase in celebrity deaths glued people together across the
globe in expressing grief and dismay and concerns regarding
who could go next.

As vehicles for asserting and affirming moral and social
norms, dead celebrities influence opinion and debate. However, dead celebrities are not all used in the same way by consumers, and they bind people together in different ways and
for different reasons. These different ways and reasons can be
encapsulated through four categories defining a dead celebrity's death: timely; tragic; tragic-foolish; and tragic-heroic.
Each category helps the consumer explore notions of morality and social norms and is consequently symbolically valuable as part of dead celebrities' posthumous careers and their
agency despite death. The first category is that of 'timely',
referring to the deaths of celebrities who have died in old
age which is considered here to entail an individual in their
late 70s onwards. They fall into the cliché of having lived to
a ripe old age and there is little surprise when their demise
is announced. Those in this category are expected or anticipated to die largely due to well-publicised ill health or simply
old age. The deaths of actress Elizabeth Taylor (79 years old,
2011), author Harper Lee (89 years old, 2016), Cuban leader
Fidel Castro (90 years old, 2016), actress and socialite Zsa
Zsa Gabor (99 years old, 2016), songwriter Leonard Cohen

(82 years old, 2016) and Sir Bruce Forsyth (89 years old, 2017) all fall into the timely category. Notably, these deaths are not classified as tragic although admittedly the lost talent or societal contribution of those in this category is often widely grieved and receives much media coverage. These timely dead celebrities provide a parable about achievement over a lifetime, some of which are positive accomplishments and contributions to society and the arts but also controversy and deviance such as multiple marriages and political views.

A large proportion of celebrity deaths fall into the 'tragic' category of dead celebrity parables. This category entails celebrities who in death gain symbolic value is as a 'body of evidence' (Foltyn, 2016) whereby the public can discuss the recklessness and downside of fame and celebrity as a parable of what morality and social norms actually should be in contrast. The tragic celebrity dead become the embodiment of unhealthy lifestyles, vanity, poor judgement, careless or stupid behaviour, or hubristic, illegal, immoral or 'sinful' activities. Essentially, they become a location of documented societal transgressions as well as overt criminal deviance including poor choices, promiscuity and sexual practices as well as drug abuse and self-endangerment. However, what is also core to these parables about morality and social norms is also the sense of underlying tragedy. The celebrity dead are not simply exemplars of how not to be or to become societal whipping boys who take the blame and punishment for broader societal failings. Instead, these well-known dead individuals become central to a sense of loss and grief; their demise is interpretable as tragedy.

Many tragic dead celebrities die young, often at the height of their fame, and are interpreted to have been cut off in their prime and their demise is therefore largely unanticipated resulting in shock. A prime example of tragic death are the members of the so-called '27 Club', which comprises celebrities (primarily musicians) who died of drug or alcohol abuse or violent means (murder or suicide) at the age of 27. Celebrities such as Janis Joplin, Jim Morrison, Kurt Cobain and Amy Winehouse have entered this club and are hailed as a tragic loss to both the world and the music scene. Other deaths interpreted principally as tragic are related to age and the stage of life the celebrity was in before death. For example, where the celebrity had a young family, such as 28-year-old actor Heath Ledger who had an infant daughter or reality television star Jade Goody who died at age 27 leaving behind two young children. Even being older but leaving a young family fulfils a sense of tragedy, particularly if the cause of death is unusual, as in the case of 44-year-old television personality Steve Irwin who died following a stingray barb piercing his heart whilst filming a documentary, leaving his wife as a widow with two small children in 2006. What unites these tragic celebrity deaths is that they were unanticipated.

Other tragic celebrity deaths are polarised for although they are unanticipated, they fail to be surprising, reflecting the assumption that celebrities can and do behave badly (Gies, 2011), often due to (but not exclusively) drug or alcohol abuse. For example, singer Whitney Houston's demise due to the effects of drug intoxication in 2012 was seen as tragic due to the loss of her singing talent and compounded by the death of her daughter Bobbi Kristina Brown in 2015, also from the effects of drug intoxication. Houston's demise was not expected but was unsurprising due to her extensive drug abuse over many years. A further example of a tragic but unsurprising death—unsurprising due to the widely publicised drug problems during his lifetime—is singer-songwriter George Michael who died in 2016. Consumers are often aware of celebrity abuses and addictions preparing them that death might occur although correct anticipation is rare. The result of such tragic celebrity deaths is that they become symbols of the potential toxicity of attaining and maintaining celebrity status but also as a key catalyst for debate surrounding societal morality. As Gies (2011) points out, public acceptance of celebrity misbehaviour varies, and heavily depends on gender and class; therefore, the level of tragedy associated with celebrity death is contingent, and some deaths are perceived as more tragic than others.

Some of the celebrity dead do not fall into the tragedy category but instead blend tragedy with foolishness and form a third category of parable or 'tragic-foolish'. The public wisdom that you should not speak ill of the dead does not seem to apply to many dead celebrities in the 'tragic-foolish' category. This is because speaking ill of the dead is acceptable if the dead individual has value as a societal whipping boy. In this role, the celebrity dead are made to bear the blame for perceived societal mistakes and failings. The celebrity dead become a convenient and valuable site to rail against the ills of society. As such, the dead celebrity in the tragic-foolish category has value as a symbol of a foolish or even immoral lifestyle or life choices that can be 'punished' on behalf of society by consumers, through criticism of their bad behaviour. This includes actress Natasha Richardson who died of a preventable skiing head injury, preventable if she had worn the recommended head protection, in 2009, or actor Paul Walker who died in a car accident caused by excessive speed in 2013. Through hindsight, the individual consumer can identify the foolish choices of the dead celebrity, and whilst acknowledging a tragedy has occurred, these celebrity deaths are useful parables against transgressing rules and making bad choices.

An exemplar of tragic-foolish celebrity death is embodied by Anna Nicole Smith who died in 2007 following an accidental overdose of prescription drugs she was taking for an infection (Foltyn, 2016). During her life, she became a celebrity as a reality star, a model including for *Playboy*, a widow of a nonagenarian oil billionaire, a grieving mother of a deceased 20-year-old son as well as mother to a 5-month-old daughter at the time of her death. The manner of Smith's death led to speculation and ultimately accusations of a variety of personal failings and immorality. She was heavily 'punished' through criticism of her life choices including her perceived gold-digging marriage, infidelity, promiscuity, vanity, exhibitionism, drug abuse, and ultimately her refusal to go to hospital when obviously ill. Smith encapsulates the ideal scenario for a tragic-foolish celebrity death and forms a posthumous career as a parable about morality through her lifestyle and choices. Smith's symbolic value as a social glue is through her death creating her as 'other' (Becker, 1963). She embodies a collapsed morality which people can unite against and be bound together in a united sense of disapproval but underpinned by the tragic loss of a mother with an infant daughter.

A fourth and final category creates a parable that combines the tragic with the heroic whereby celebrity individuals die during a valorous deed or doing something dangerous, adventurous or ground-breaking. This category, therefore, includes dead celebrities such as Formula One racing driver Ayrton Senna who died in a high-speed accident during the 1994 San Marino Grand Prix and aviation pioneer Amelia Earhart, who was the first female aviator to fly solo across the Atlantic Ocean but disappeared and was presumed dead in 1937 while flying over the Pacific Ocean. A particularly strong instance of the tragic-heroic is Captain Robert Falcon Scott who died with his team on the return journey from the South Pole in 1912. The discovery of the latter's diary after his death has immortalised the tragic expedition and granted Scott agency in death allowing him to speak from beyond the grave. It was Scott who posthumously endorsed the heroism of his ill and weakened colleague Captain Lawrence

Oates, who voluntarily left the tent and walked to his death, reportedly saying, 'I am just going outside and may be some time'. He recorded in his diary, 'We knew that poor Oates was walking to his death, but though we tried to dissuade him, we knew it was the act of a brave man and an English gentleman.'[2] Scott's posthumous celebrity career as a symbol of valour and tragedy was only consolidated by the inspiring 'Message to the Public' that he recorded in his diary, which was later published where he wrote:

> We took risks, we knew we took them; things
> have come out against us, and therefore we have
> no cause for complaint, but bow to the will of
> Providence, determined still to do our best to the
> last ... Had we lived, I should have had a tale to
> tell of the hardihood, endurance, and courage
> of my companions which would have stirred the
> heart of every Englishman. These rough notes
> and our dead bodies must tell the tale, but surely,
> surely, a great rich country like ours will see
> that those who are dependent on us are properly
> provided for.[3]

Scott successfully achieves a posthumous career as a valuable social symbol. He, like other tragic-heroic dead celebrities, attains agency as a symbol of aspiration to the living, not to die tragically, but to strive beyond limitations and social norms to achieve greatness on behalf of humankind.

These four dead celebrity categories formulate parables with different messages but all highlight that symbolic value is firmly connected with affirmation or a challenge to societally-shared morality and social norms. Consequently, these categories have a direct influence on the symbolic worth of dead celebrity posthumous careers and ultimately upon their economic value.

CELEBRITY DEAD EARNERS

Dead celebrity posthumous careers extend beyond being symbolically influential as contemporary parables. In fact, being dead can be a very financially lucrative career move particularly as death entails the end of a physical body but not the death of the image left behind. The image of the dead celebrity can range from photographs to cartoons and from music they performed and wrote to movies in which they acted. This legacy of visual and audio material prevents dead celebrities from disappearing from social life. As such, dead celebrities continue to exist through the concept of continuing bonds, which are commonly used to analyse relationships between the living and the dead and to trace a lack of such relationships. Dead celebrities are granted a social life (and posthumous career) through the bonds that make them 'matter here and now in various respects' and so do not endure a post-mortem social death (Jonsson, 2015: 284). Through continuing bonds, dead celebrities have the ability to sustain their commercial and symbolic value after death, often transitioning into iconic status. As an icon, dead celebrities become regarded as a representative symbol or at least worthy of veneration. They become frozen in time with continuing bonds linking them to the global public, particularly as the agency of the dead celebrities allows them to continue in new commercial exploits. This is particularly apparent via product endorsement where long-dead icons of the silver screen, including Audrey Hepburn, Marilyn Monroe and Steve McQueen sell us chocolate, perfume and cars. The celebrity dead even sell us pens with luxury pen-maker Montblanc having a 'muses' line showcasing Ingrid Bergman, Greta Garbo, Princess Grace of Monaco and Marlene Dietrich[4]. Notably the agency of the celebrity dead is interpreted here as the ability to continue performing and producing 'new' products albeit through state-of-the-art audio and visual technologies and with permission from the dead celebrity's family or agent who 'own' their estate and legacy.

Product endorsements are just one component of celebrity posthumous careers with many dead celebrities having the agency to continue performing. Some music stars even return to the stage after their death. This happened when a 1912 concert grand player piano with rolls that preserved Gershwin's keystrokes performed at a centennial concert marking his death (Kearl, 2010). As part of the performance, a spotlight moved across the stage as if the spectral presence of Gershwin had walked to the piano to play and where a glass of wine was provided for him. There was a divided response to the Natalie Cole's recording of 'Unforgettable' with her dead father Nat King Cole's vocals, especially when it won a Grammy for Best Album of the Year in 1991. However, in 1992, when she performed the song with Nat King Cole appearing on a screen behind her, there was little controversy (Brunt, 2015). Accusations of musical necrophilia have continued despite claims that sincere tributes are being made by using past artists, particularly Elvis Presley, to perform alongside contemporary living artists. There may be ethical dilemmas over using dead musicians' past vocals, but this is compounded when they also visually perform. When, in 2014, Michael Jackson took to the stage as a hologram fans were left both thrilled and uncomfortable. Imagining a star's presence or seeing and hearing a recording of the dead differs from live performers interacting with a hologram of the recently deceased.

Posthumous performing is not limited to music but also extends into film with both long-dead and more recently dead actors appearing in cameos and minor roles in films. *Rogue One* (2016), the standalone film set in the Star Wars Universe, featured British actor Peter Cushing who died in

1994 in a speaking role whereby his face was imposed by CGI on a live actor. Much angry and critical discussion followed regarding this use of the dead[5]. Carrie Fisher also appeared as her 19-year-old self from the original *Star Wars: A New Hope* (1977), and her appearance had particular resonance as she died during the opening weeks of the cinematic release of *Rogue One*. Viewers were faced with the youthful Fisher knowing she was dead (and had approved of her CGI cameo) and aware that her 60-year-old self was in post-production for the next Star Wars instalment due in 2017.

Celebrities' financially lucrative posthumous careers have become so significant that *Forbes* (business magazine) began releasing a yearly Top Earning Dead Celebrities list[6] in 2001 (*see* D'Rozario and Bryant, 2013; D'Rozario, 2016). Often referred to as the Dead Rich List (terminology adopted here), it is a direct reflection of the yearly *Forbes* Rich List that reveals the wealthiest people in the world. Over 54 names (of which notably only four are women) have appeared on the Dead Rich List since its inception, with some appearing only once or twice, whilst others are present each year and several dominate the top three positions repeatedly. Michael Jackson has topped the Dead Rich List since his death in 2009 when his earnings reached $170 million resulting in him having posthumously earned more money than any single living artist in 2012 (see Fig. 1). But his earnings and agency did not end in 2012. Admittedly, in 2015, Jackson dropped to a mere $115 million, which was not much less than the nearest live music performers Katy Perry at $135 million and One Direction at $130 million in the same year (take note these earnings are related to their intensive touring rather than sales of albums). However, in 2016, Jackson enjoyed a meteoric rise in earnings to $825 million. This incredible increase in economic wealth is directly related to the sale of his half of the Sony/ATV music publishing catalogue, famous for its

2009	$90 million	(3rd place)
2010	$275 million	(1st place)
2011	$170 million	(1st place)
2012	$145 million	(2nd place)
2013	$160 million	(1st place)
2014	$140 million	(1st place)
2015	$115 million	(1st place)
2016	$825 million	(1st place)
2017	$75 million	(1st place)

Fig. 1.   Michael Jackson Posthumous Earnings (*source*: *Forbes* Dead Rich List)

ownership of much of the Beatles music, for $750 million. Interestingly, if you remove this huge one-off influx, Jackson still earned $75 million which would have left him at the top of the Dead Rich List, with the second biggest earner Charles Schultz, the creator of the *Peanuts* cartoons, earning a mere $48 million. To dethrone Jackson from being the top-earning dead celebrity is not a simple task, and there is little sign of a rival dead celebrity who could topple him in the near future.

The *Forbes* Dead Rich List reveals a number of significant trends relating to dead celebrity top earners and their posthumous careers. Firstly, when a major celebrity dies and enters the *Forbes* Dead Rich List, the first two years after death are generally the most financially successful. This earning potential is affected by what time of year the celebrity dies, as *Forbes* looks at earnings over 12 months dating from October of a given year, and also due to the deceased's estate being liquidated. For example, Elizabeth Taylor died in 2011, and her earnings peaked in the year after her death (see Fig. 2); she even managed to oust Jackson from the top of the *Forbes*

2011	$12 million	(5th place)
2012	$210 million	(1st place)
2013	$25 million	(4th place)
2014	$25 million	(4th place)
2015	$20 million	(5th place)
2016	$8 million	(13th place)
2017	$8 million	(12th place)

Fig. 2.   Elizabeth Taylor Posthumous Earnings (*source*:
Forbes Dead Rich List)

list in 2012, which is the only time this has happened since
2010 (the first year Jackson's posthumous earnings were over
a 12-month period). This peak in earnings followed the sale of
the actress' estate in 2012 which included jewellery, costumes
and art, such as an 1889 Van Gogh painting that sold for
$16 million, and property sales. It also included residuals from
Taylor's movies (i.e., after *Cleopatra*, she negotiated a 10 percent ownership stake in each of her films) and her perfume,
White Diamonds, which was a best-selling product in 2011.

Following 2012, Taylor's commercial value and posthumous career declined stabilising at around $20–25 million for
three years before witnessing a large downward shift in 2016,
which has continued into 2017. With a rise in more substantial Dead Celebrity Earners with stable posthumous economic
value, it is likely that Taylor will remain in the lower rankings
of Dead Rich List. Without the money from the sale of her
estate, she is unable to rival Jackson again. Jackson, unlike
Taylor, has his posthumous career sustained by steady revenue streams including from the successful Cirque Du Soleil
show *The Immortal Tour*.

A second trend in the Dead Rich list is the ranking of the
dead celebrity and the longevity that is, or is not, achieved on

the list. Taylor's ranking has gone into decline since her death whereas other stars, such as Elvis Presley, demonstrate an enduring posthumous career of immense commercial value, ensuring a high ranking on the Dead Rich List. Presley's posthumous success is linked to revenue streams, such as his home, Graceland, which remains a top tourist destination, licensing and merchandise deals relating to his image as well as ownership of a library of music similar to Jackson's Sony/ATV music publishing catalogue. Since 2001, Presley has dominated the *Forbes* Dead Rich List (see Fig. 3) holding first or second place up until 2008.

2001	\$35 million	(1st place)
2002	\$37 million	(1st place)
2003	\$40 million	(1st place)
2004	\$40 million	(1st place)
2005	\$45 million	(1st place)
2006	\$42 million	(2nd place)
2007	\$49 million	(1st place)
2008	\$52 million	(1st place)
2009	\$55 million	(4th place)
2010	\$60 million	(2nd place)
2011	\$55 million	(2nd place)
2012	\$55 million	(3rd place)
2013	\$55 million	(2nd place)
2014	\$55 million	(2nd place)
2015	\$55 million	(2nd place)
2016	\$27 million	(4th place)
2017	\$35 million	(4th place)

Fig. 3.   Elvis Presley Posthumous Earnings (*source*: *Forbes* Dead Rich List)

Dislodging Presley from the top earnings list has only been achieved once before 2009. This was by Kurt Cobain who reached the top spot for a single year in 2006. This sudden rise in affluence was connected to Cobain's widow Courtney Love selling his 25 percent stake in his band's song catalogue to *Primary Wave*, a New York music publishing company for a reported $50 million[7]. Presley's apparent dramatic drop to fourth place in 2016 on the Dead Rich List suggests a 50 percent drop in earnings between 2015–2016. However, *Forbes* admits that this shift is due to a change in how it accounts for Graceland ticket sales rather than plummeting commercial value of Presley. 2017 saw an increase in Presley's earnings due to two new openings within Graceland—The Guesthouse Hotel and Elvis Presley's Memphis Entertainment Complex—but it was still not enough to move up from fourth place. It would seem that although the King of Rock 'n' Roll still has significant commercial value and a secure posthumous career in the future, he is going to struggle to stay in the top three on the Dead Rich List.

The *Forbes* Dead Rich list illustrates how the agency of dead celebrities maintains posthumous careers that can be commercially successful. However, it is getting harder to achieve a position amongst the top 10 dead celebrity earners on the Dead Rich List with last place still requiring earnings of $10 in 2015 and $11 million in 2016. Dead celebrity posthumous careers are witnessing a dramatic earnings influx making it harder not only to become a top earner but even harder to be a consistent top earner. 2016 saw two key newcomers onto the top earning dead celebrity list in the form of Prince who entered at number five earning $25 million and David Bowie at number 11 earning $10.5 million. Whether either of these musicians will rival Jackson in the future or whether they will attain earning longevity like Presley remains to be seen. However, both musicians had substantial posthumous career earnings in 2016 even though neither had earnings for a complete 12 months. This impressive income reflected Prince's successful live music shows in 2016 before his death and his album sales, which at 2.5 million albums was more than any other dead musician and Bowie's *Blackstar* album being released just two days before his death. It is speculation whether they will continue to hold places on the *Forbes* Dead Rich List in the future, but this is likely, due to their estimated revenue streams that will continue posthumously. The *Forbes* Dead Rich list illustrates that for many celebrity individuals being dead has substantially boosted their economic value aiding them in actively maintaining commercially viable posthumous careers. Being dead does not undermine celebrities as a consumable good and can, in fact, make them more consumable and exceed their economic value in life. For example, Jackson's posthumous career has made him the most financially successful recording artist, alive or dead, in history. However, where there is death and wealth, there are potential beneficiaries. Who benefits from or 'owns' the celebrity dead and their agency via their posthumous career can become a contentious issue.

OWNING THE CELEBRITY DEAD

When you die, your assets pass on to your next of kin who are your direct relatives or whoever is specified in a will. You can leave your house, money, jewellery, even your pets, to your loved ones. However, your image, namely how you look and sound, is a complex issue especially when you are a celebrity, and it is the most valuable asset you own. Frank Sinatra sang 'I'm Gonna Live till I Die' but his career did not end with his death. Instead, for Sinatra, his posthumous career reflected another of his famous songs, that for him, like many celebrities, 'The Best is Yet to Come', especially if you own the dead. Owning dead celebrities can be hugely financial valuable and inherently simpler as in death celebrities stop being volatile or demanding. They are, for all intents and purposes, predictable and their behaviour contained by being dead. The celebrity dead cannot do anything to change the bond forged by death with the consumer although admittedly posthumous exposés may reveal an aspect of their life that may cause a shift in consumer opinions (Cashmore, 2014). Dead celebrities' posthumous careers benefit from being talked about and remaining in the public eye, and after death exposés can be useful to this process of remaining active and visible in celebrity culture. Admittedly, there are exceptions to this rule, with some celebrity posthumous exposés being damaging or even ending posthumous careers. For example, UK television personality and charity fundraiser Jimmy Savile whose death in 2011 led to a plethora of public grief and an estimated 5,000 mourners paying tribute to his gold coffin, which lay in state in the Queen's Hotel, Leeds[8]. However, when in 2012 sexual abuse by Savile became public, his value as a celebrity was tainted as he became 'notorious' (Penfold-Mounce, 2009), and his assets were frozen by executors in anticipation of victims making claims for damages. Savile's agency in death was through what Furedi (2013) described as a crisis of authority and a subsequent moral crusade regarding sex abuse. Ultimately, the exposure of Savile contests the expression that 'no publicity is bad publicity' and that a change to consumer opinion of dead celebrities can truly be a nail in the coffin of their posthumous career, but it did not prevent the agency of the dead.

Apart from exceptional cases, such as Savile, the celebrity dead are far easier to manage, and have their agency directed towards their commercial value, maximising them as a brand. As Barron (2014) writes the economics of celebrity whether they are dead or alive reflects the dominant spirit of capital-ism established in the 1980s in the Western world. Whilst live celebrities seek to enhance their profitability, celebrity culture has developed to support this by spanning companies and services that seek celebrities to endorse and create consumable goods. Celebrity is a potent force for inspiring people to consume, and this potency does not end with death. Death opens up new avenues through which posthumous careers can thrive, even for people whose celebrity status is not rooted in film, television or music. For example, Charles Schultz, the creator of *Peanuts*, has consistently been in the top three top-earning dead celebrities since the inception of the Dead Rich List in 2001. Even JRR Tolkien, the author of *The Lord of the Rings*, has appeared on the Dead Rich list in the early 2000s due to the successful Peter Jackson film franchise. Meanwhile, scientist Albert Einstein continues a vibrant posthumous career outside of the scientific community via his own range of T-shirts, posters, tablets and the licencing of his name to Baby Einstein products.

Notably, posthumous careers of the celebrity dead do not continue of their own volition. Although the dead have agency, it needs to be directed and managed, which is achieved by the living who own the dead celebrity. The rise of the advertising and marketing industry in the 20th century alongside a globalised celebrity culture and mass entertainment via multiple media and social media forms has been a principle factor in the rush to benefit from the value of dead celebrities. It has also produced a need to create a legal framework to address conflict over ownership of the abstract namely the celebrity dead and their legacy and potential posthumous career. Exerting control over the intangible is complex and a whole speciality of law, namely intellectual property, which has developed to deal with controversy that commonly occurs over ownership of films, computer programs, inventions, designs and marks of traders for their goods or services and literary and artistic words (Bainbridge, 2002: 3). However, intellectual property also includes more abstract ownership, such as a phrase in a song or a musical riff, coming up with a certain idea or the look and feel of a computer game, an individual's image or even body parts and genetic material (Halbert, 1999: ix). The latter two are of particular interest in the instance of owning a dead celebrity; for to own a celebrity individual's image or body parts and genetic material is to own a potentially profitable asset if managed correctly.

Ownership of dead celebrities has opened a range of issues beyond those experienced by celebrities in life. The celebrity dead as intellectual property alongside their physical estate is an asset, which is most commonly passed to their direct relatives on their death. However, in some instances, the celebrity dead have endured major and sustained legal battles over who will own their posthumous career and none more so than Jimi Hendrix. In 1995, Jimi Hendrix's father Al won back control of his son's estimated $80 million legacy from lawyer Leo Branton who had been sold the right to manage Jimi's estate (and, therefore, his posthumous career) shortly after his death. Branton's success in managing Hendrix's career after death led to tension with Hendrix's family who had not fully appreciated the value of their dead celebrity relative. A legal battle eventually led to Al Hendrix reacquiring the ownership and control of the Jimi Hendrix industry comprising copyrights on his entire recorded output, unreleased tapes, music publishing rights, photos, films, videos, and the right to exploit his image. However, controversy over owning and controlling Hendrix's posthumous career began again after the death of Al in 2002. Hendrix's siblings Janie and Leon Hendrix entered into a conflict as the former was granted sole control of Jimi's estate and intellectual property rights and, therefore, his posthumous career. Leon unsuccessfully contested their father's will (2004–2007) and then fought a legal battle with Janie (2009–2015) due to copyright infringement of the guitarist's image on merchandise, as Leon's company had printed shirts and other merchandise with Jimi's image and signature without permission[9]. The Hendrix case highlights that owning the celebrity dead and financially benefitting from their continuing career is lucrative but can lead to bitter conflict and the testing of family kinship ties.

Conflict over ownership of dead celebrities is not just over who receives the financial rewards but also regarding how and what the dead celebrities do as part of their posthumous career. For example, James Dean's family have been criticised for exploiting his agency in a manner with which the wider public, particularly fans, do not agree. Selling Dean's image to many companies for product endorsement, including Lee Jeans, has led to accusations of unscrupulous profiteering and a lack of selective association with products and services. However, his symbolic value as an icon of rebellion still carries weight as illustrated by him appearing in an advert (or a least an actor playing Dean) for a South African investment company. The viewer is shown Dean surviving the car crash, which killed him in 1955 at age 24 and challenged to consider 'given more time. Imagine the possibilities.' The advert received critical acclaim and was hailed by film critic Barry Ronge as 'the smartest use of a celebrity we have seen in a decade'[10]. Dean's family may have been criticised by fans for how it has directed his posthumous career, but it remains the key beneficiaries of his continuing commercial success, rooted in his enduring symbolic value.

Fred Astaire's posthumous career has also led to division within his family with his widow Robyn Astaire becoming an ardent guardian of her husband's image following his death in 1987. As the agent of her husband's posthumous career, she sought to control how and by whom his image was used.

She denied permission for clips to be used in a 1992 tribute to Ginger Rogers whilst production on 1994's *That's Entertainment! III* was delayed following her demands for payment for her husband's scenes, and in 1989, she sued Best Film & Video for using 90 seconds of Astaire footage, taking the case to the US Supreme Court. Controversially, she did grant permission for his image from the 1951 film *Royal Wedding* to be used in an advertisement for Dirt Devil Vacuums in 1997. This led to family strife with Fred Astaire's daughter Ava Astaire-McKenzie who voiced her disapproval, saying she was 'saddened that after Fred's wonderful career, he was sold to the devil'[11]. Robyn's defence to this disapproval revolved around her belief that it was what Astaire would have wanted due to her financial insecurity as a direct result of prosecuting infringers of his (and, therefore, legally her) intellectual property. Being a guardian and defender of a posthumous celebrity career is an expensive process leading to potential sacrifices in how the dead celebrity is used in order to meet legal costs.

Celebrity posthumous careers not only reveal family and legal conflict over the ownership of the dead and their posthumous career income but also the rise of an industry specifically targeting the management of dead celebrities. This industry is defined by companies specialising in working with and for the celebrity dead. In this context, these companies will be referred to as 'owning' or 'owners' of dead celebrities although often (but not always) they are employed by family to manage celebrity posthumous careers rather than being the exclusive owner. Ownership is, therefore, often control and management of a dead celebrity career as an agent or brand manager on behalf of dead celebrities' families. Their role is to improve and maintain the career of the dead celebrity through effective management, thereby maximising the earnings of the celebrity dead. Authentic Brands Group[12] (ABG) is a key example of a company, which owns the celebrity dead.

According to its website, it 'owns, manages, and elevates the long-term value of a portfolio of global brands. We are a brand development, marketing, and entertainment company'[13]. In this role, it owns a number of high-profile dead celebrities, including Elvis Presley and golfer Bobby Jones, as well as live ones such as basketball star Shaquille O'Neal, singer and actress Thalia and also fashion and sports brands. The company tagline 'We are brand owners. Curators. Guardians'[14] iterates not only their role as owners but also their intent to be keepers or custodians who will guard and protect these brands. The tagline conveys that dead celebrity brands need to be protected from people seeking to use and financially benefit to the detriment of the brand and brand owner. ABG projects itself as the defender and protector of the dead, who are vulnerable to being exploited by others. It is the mouthpiece and manager of the dead signed to their care and is there to protect and maintain the agency of the celebrity dead.

ABG promises to 'achieve brand efficiencies through a synergistic marketing approach that goes across social and digital media, print, OOH [Out of home advertising], in-store, ecommerce, creative, editorial and PR [public relations].'[15] This shift towards brand efficiency and the commercial success of dead celebrities and their posthumous careers is illustrated by the purchase of the rights or rather the ownership of Marilyn Monroe in 2011. Monroe has, following this shift in posthumous career ownership, become incredibly productive for someone who has been dead since 1962. In fact, her agency has been noted, leading to the observation that she 'remains the most alive dead person in history, rivalled only by Princess Diana' (Cashmore, 2014: 58). In 2015 alone, she appeared in *Coca-Cola* adverts (alongside Elvis Presley), *Max Factor* and *Dior* perfume (with Grace Kelly and Marlene Dietrich). Monroe has also had a clothing line inspired by her

with US retailer Macy's and has been made into an animated
character called Mini Marilyn who

> empowers girls, encouraging them to be confident,
> take risks and dream big. She seeks to make the
> world a better place by inspiring others through her
> creative mindset and individuality, delivering the
> message that no matter how little you are you can
> achieve great things.[16]

Mini Marilyn is designed with a particular purpose.
Firstly, to serve as an 'engine for licensing, retail and other
brand opportunities'[17] particularly in film, TV, video games
and live venue attractions. Secondly, it targets millennials
aged between 17–34[18], and finally, it has a major appeal to the
Chinese market. Inspired by Monroe, Mini Marilyn stands to
make her dead celebrity muse into a global icon beyond what
she achieved in life and even in her posthumous career so far.

Given the rise in the professionalization of owning dead
celebrities and the possibility of conflict and even misman-
agement by direct relatives, a new development has occurred
regarding celebrity posthumous careers since 2014. The suicide of actor and comedian Robin Williams in August 2014
has become the first case of a celebrity, whilst alive, very
directly and explicitly managing his posthumous career. It is
most likely that Williams' intention in the revision of his 2012
trust was to avoid estate tax value of his celebrity 'right of
publicity'[19] rather than to use his agency to curb his posthumous career; however, this is what he achieved. The right
of publicity, which lies at the heart of Williams controlling
his career whilst dead, refers to key components of celebrity image, in the form of their name, likeness, voice, signa-
ture and photograph. These components of celebrity image
(upon which much of celebrity careers are based) is legally
recognised as property even after death and in California

this recognition is for up to 70 years. Therefore, this right of publicity creates a significant window for a financially advantageous celebrity posthumous career to flourish. However, before his death, Williams safeguarded his posthumous career by including in a deed held by The Robin Williams Trust a detailed description outlining how he intended to be used in any publicity. By passing his right of publicity to the Windfall Foundation, a qualified charity set up in his name, there is an unlimited estate tax deduction for money or property. This meant it did not matter whether Williams' right of publicity was worth a few hundred dollars or millions as it was protected from any litigation from the Internal Revenue Service regarding the value of the right of publicity and the estate tax that would be owed[20].

There is only speculation and confusion regarding why Williams granted the financially valuable right of publicity to the Windfall Foundation and then forbade it from using the rights until August 2039. This does not prevent films in which he had starred from being shown, but it prevents his name and image from being used in advertisements and stops him from being inserted digitally into new television shows or films. It is unlikely to ever be clear as to why Williams did what he did, but what it demonstrates is that celebrities can plan and manage their own posthumous career before they die. In doing like Williams, celebrities do not have to pass over full control of their posthumous career to their family or a brand management company and trust they will act in a way of which the celebrities would have approved. Instead, dead celebrities can remain in control and exert their agency for themselves by leaving strict instructions regarding how they wish their posthumous career to be conducted. For Williams, it would seem the genie is truly free, i.e., free from other people controlling his posthumous career other than how he specified in life. He owns his posthumous career in death and has limited the caretakers of his rights of publicity on the terms he desired. However, after 2039, Williams' posthumous career is more precarious as the Windfall Foundation will be able to exploit the rights of publicity. Williams has set a precedent in how to own a posthumous career from beyond the grave, but it remains to be seen how many other celebrities will follow his example.

CONCLUSION

Death is not the end but a new phase for celebrity careers. In a mass-mediated, technology-driven global world, a remarkable situation has occurred, whereby the dead no longer remain silent as the grave. They become a valuable commodity to be owned and exchanged allowing the celebrities dead to wield agency to the extent that they can speak and keep working after death. The actual body of celebrities has become less necessary than before. This is because once celebrities are audibly or visually recorded, they may as well be dead as they can continue without a body via a posthumous career (Giles, 2017). The value of dead celebrities and their continuing posthumous careers can be as symbolically powerful parables, economically valuable product endorsers, or even holographic performers. This value encapsulates how capitalism and consumerism is so entrenched in the Western world that death is now just a new stage in a celebrity's career path. Cashmore (2014: 59) claims that Marilyn Monroe was the first celebrity death leading to renewal and beatification, but she is certainly not the last. She has been a catalyst in the trend for posthumous careers that has led to those who have died before Monroe to be resurrected and begin working again despite being dead. Dead celebrity posthumous careers mark out new boundaries for existence. Being dead has significant symbolic and commercial value meaning that an individual can have a life *in* death and not just a life after death. In the next chapter the agency of the dead is examined as symbolically valuable and powerful in exploring cultural beliefs about death through the myths association with the transplantation of organs and body parts from the dead.

NOTES

1. Donnelly, G. (2009, 15 May) Question time with Jonathan Rhys Meyers http://www.dailymail.co.uk/femail/article-1180855/Question-time-Jonathan-Rhys-Meyers.html[accessed 23/08/2017]

2. Scott Last Expedition – RF Scott's Diary, Scott Polar Research Institute http://www.spri.cam.ac.uk/museum/diaries/scottslastexpedition/1912/03/17/friday-march-16th-or-saturday-17th-1912/ [accessed 23/08/2017]

3. Scott's Last Expedition – RF Scott's Diary, Scott Polar Research Institute http://www.spri.cam.ac.uk/museum/diaries/scottslastexpedition/1912/03/29/message-to-the-public/[accessed 23/08/2017]

4. Shoard, C. (2016, December 21). Peter Cushing is dead. Rogue One's resurrection is a digital indignity. https://www.theguardian.com/commentisfree/2016/dec/21/peter-cushing-rogue-one-resurrection-cgi[accessed 12/10/2017]

5. http://www.montblanc.com/en-gb/collection/limited-editions/muses-edition.html?=undefined[accessed 22/8/2017]

6. http://www.forbes.com/sites/zackomalleygreenburg/2016/10/12/the-highest-paid-dead-celebrities-of-2016/#773955a18d2e [accessed 24/01/2017]

7. http://www.forbes.com/2006/10/20/tech-media_06 deadcelebs_cx_pf_top-earning-dead-celebrities.html [accessed 26/01/2017]

8. Wainwright, M. (2011, November 8) Jimmy Savile 'lies in state' as 5,000 file past his coffin to pay their last respects. *The Guardian*. https://www.theguardian.com/tv-and-radio/2011/nov/08/jimmy-savile-coffin-public-display. [accessed 27/01/2017].

9. Anon. (2011, November 9) Sir Jimmy Savile's funeral takes place at Leeds Cathedral. *BBC News*. http://www.bbc.co.uk/news/uk-england-leeds-15647363 [accessed 27/07/2017]

10. Kreps, D. (2015, August 15) Jimi Hendrix's Estate Settles Licensing Legal Battle. *Rolling Stone*.http://www.rollingstone.com/music/news/jimi-hendrixs-siblings-settle-licensing-legal-battle-20150815[accessed 27/01/2017]

11. Smith, D. (2009, September 21) James Dean lives on in South African-made TV commercial. *The Guardian*. https://www.theguardian.com/media/2009/sep/21/james-dean-television-commercial-advertisement[accessed 23/08/2017]

12. Anon. (1999, June 18) Fred Astaire's last dance: The famed dancer died 12 years ago, and the battle of his work began. *Entertainment Weekly*. http://www.ew.com/article/1999/06/18/fred-astaires-last-dance [accessed 16/9/2016]

13. http://authenticbrandsgroup.com/ [accessed 27/01/2017]

14. http://authenticbrandsgroup.com/what-we-do/ [accessed 27/01/2017]

15. http://authenticbrandsgroup.com/ [accessed 27/01/2017]

16. http://authenticbrandsgroup.com/what-we-do/ [accessed 27/01/2017]

17. http://marilynmonroe.com/mini-marilyn/ [accessed 27/01/2017]

18. Frater, P. (2015, April 9) China's DMG Teams with Authentic Brands to Launch Mini Marilyn Character. *Variety*. http://variety.com/2015/biz/asia/chinas-dmg-teams-with-authentic-brands-to-launch-mini-marilyn-character-1201469245/ [accessed 27/01/2017]

19. Young, VM. (2015, April 9) Authentic Brands Group Introduces Mini Marilyn. *Women's Wear Daily (WDD)*. http://wwd.com/business-news/marketing-promotion/authentic-brands-group-introduces-mini-marilyn-10109393/ [accessed 27/01/2017]

20. Anon. (2015, May 26) 4 Lessons from The Robin Williams Estate Litigation. *LAW 360*. https://www.law360.com/articles/659532/4-lessons-from-the-robin-williams-estate-litigation [accessed 27/01/2017]

21. Anon. (2015, May 26) 4 Lessons from The Robin Williams Estate Litigation. *LAW 360*. https://www.law360.com/articles/659532/4-lessons-from-the-robin-williams-estate-litigation[accessed 27/01/2017]

3

THE AFTERLIFE OF CORPSES: ORGAN TRANSPLANTATION

The value of the dead, economically and symbolically, varies across time, place and culture. In June 2014, a Dutch man, Leo Bonten, has his leg surgically removed. He successfully fought the hospital that amputated his leg over its ownership saying

> My leg is my property. People keep kidney stones in a jar on the mantelpieces. Ashes of dead people are included in tattoos. I'm going to make a lamp of my leg[1]

Bonten had the limb preserved and turned into a lamp where the leg was placed in formaldehyde inside a large cylindrical container. Claiming that it helped him to deal with the loss, Bonten planned to sell the leg lamp in order to pay his medical bills before facing problems due to the legalities surrounding the buying and selling of human body parts. The value of an amputated limb, in this instance, is economic and symbolic to the individual involved, but there is also a wider societal value. The question of body part ownership (namely organs or limbs) is raised along with what is and is not an acceptable object, i.e. a preserved limb as a lamp. Even fake leg lamps are contentious as illustrated in *A Christmas Story* (1983) where a disembodied shapely leg (admittedly, it is not suggested to be a real leg) lamp features prominently in the story as a source of conflict between a husband and wife. Retaining parts of the human corpse has an extensive and macabre history as illustrated by people collecting criminal body parts or even entire skeletons as trophies or souvenirs or criminals keeping bits of their victims (Penfold-Mounce, 2010). Such ghoulish collections have become popularly consumed via the most famous of limbs and organ trophy-takers, American necrophile Ed Gein. Buffalo Bill from Thomas Harris's *The Silence of the Lambs* was based on Gein and his penchant for exhuming bodies and making items from the corpses including lampshades and seat covers, bedposts decorations, soup bowls and even a female body suit.

What these disturbing examples demonstrate is that pieces of the dead can have agency via a second life or rather an afterlife. When the original body has died, pieces of the dead can have life in a new way, ranging from macabre objects, such as furniture and souvenirs to saving the life of another person through organ transplantation. Organs and limbs can exist beyond the death of the original owner as bio-objects, a concept used to understand the process and boundaries wherein life-forms or living entities are first made into objects, which then challenge social and cultural boundaries. In this instance, donated organs and limbs become bio-objects 'through scientific labor and its associated technologies, and then come to be attributed with specific identities' (Holmberg, Schwennesen and Webster, 2011: 740), different from their original identity as part of a particular living person. In this chapter, the focus on the afterlife of the dead as bio-objects will be examined through the mythology surrounding organ transplantation representations within popular culture. Representation of corpses as a whole or in pieces within popular culture grants a new mode of value and agency as they transition from one life to another. The afterlife will be used in this context rather than as a posthumous life because it encapsulated the idea of a realm where an essential part of an individual's identity or consciousness continues to exist after death. This relationship between organs' identity and a new owner leading to conflict is central to the chapter's argument about the dead possessing agency. The afterlife of the corpse in bits, namely via organ donation, where they have a new life and identity is a stark contrast to posthumous celebrity careers where the well-known dead live on as themselves (see Chapter 2).

An immense range of scholarship exists about organ transplantation from a medical and psychological approach much of which is published in books and medical journals that are devoted solely to this topic. There has also been much interdisciplinary consideration of global organ donation rates and the problem of insufficient organs being donated to meet the need, the ethics of transplantation (Cameron & Hoffenberg, 1999; Delmonico, Arnold, Scheper-Hughes, Siminoff, Kahn, & Youngner, 2002) and organ trafficking (Budiani-Saberi & Delmonico, 2008; Nullis-Kapp, 2004; Francis & Francis, 2010). Organ transplantation has also been considered via its relationship with television and film representation, ranging from exploration of its impact on public understanding of organ donation and transplantation (Morgan, Harrison, Chewning, Davis, & DiCorcia, 2007); on organ donation rates (Morgan, King, Smith, & Ivic, 2010); and on donors and non-donors' knowledge, attitudes and behaviours (Morgan, Movius & Cody, 2009). However, apart from O'Neill's (2006) work on organ transplantation myths in popular culture, there is very limited exploration of the symbolic value of organs being harvested from the dead and their use as a narrative tool examining social fears about the body and death. This chapter seeks to fill the research gap within organ transplantation literature by considering the agency of the dead through their symbolic value in enduring Western popular culture mythology surrounding organ transplantation. Organ transplantation in this context will refer to organs harvested from deceased donors and will focus predominantly on hearts and eyes. This afterlife of corpse bits as bio-objects will be explored through the tales that have become a mythology surrounding organ transplantation and which are disseminated and reiterated by popular culture. Death will be highlighted as a new beginning for corpse bits, not only with their value to a recipient of an organ transplant as their life is extended but also as a valuable symbolic tool to encapsulate and explore wider cultural and societal fears about identity, control, inequality and trust.

THE ROOTS OF TRANSPLANTATION MYTHOLOGY

Mythology is a key feature of every culture. Attempts to explain myths include human societies expressing fundamental feelings in common, such as love, hate, rage; explanations of phenomena that are not understood; providing accounts of historical events; or explanations of traditional cultural rituals. No matter which explanation is true, myth is a valuable storytelling tool that engages with fact and fiction and explores commonly held fears and ideas. Organ donation and transplantation has a mythology dating back to before it was medically possible and is rooted in deeply held cultural beliefs about the body and bodily integrity. These cultural beliefs constitute not only explanations and meanings but also an ideology meaning certain political and economic realities are legitimated

(Lindenbaum & Lock, 1993). In the case of medicine and its ability to allow organ and limb transplantation, these cultural beliefs are rooted in accounts of selective medical knowledge, demonstrating 'the manner in which social interest becomes seamlessly incorporated in the set of tacit assumptions about reality' (Comaroff, 1982: 50). The catalyst for transplantation myths lies within the classic gothic novel *Frankenstein* by Mary Wollstonecraft Shelley, published in 1818. *Frankenstein* lies at the heart of transplantation myths origins which have become used as a springboard to explore fearful cultural beliefs of the possible afterlife of body parts. Wollstonecraft Shelley was writing at a time when transplantation was impossible. However, her work laid a foundation for Western transplantation mythology to concentrate on fear and the monstrous and which has lingered on into the era where organ transplantation has become feasible.

The themes of the Frankenstein monster influenced transplantation mythology are the dark side of science rooted in superstition and anxiety. This is where man is playing God and science is out of control breeding a distrust of doctors (O'Neill, 2006). But this leads to the question of why has this Frankenstein myth been so very powerful and fundamental to all transplantation mythology since? O'Neill (2006: 223) addresses this question arguing that

> It is powerful because it meets the essential elements required for a story to become a myth…. the story must endure through time; …must be taken up and reproduced by others in multiple forms; …develop a life of its own; and …must become a symbol that is widely and immediately meaningful in certain contexts.

The continual release and evolution of representations of the Frankenstein-rooted mythology in popular culture reinforces the cultural fears it portrays in the collective consciousness. It informs and influences consumers and shapes views of transplantation leading to an extensive (mis)education (Morgan et al., 2007). Although much has been done to improve attitudes and knowledge about the realities of organ donation and to debunk myths and urban legends, such as via the UK's National Health Service (NHS) organ donation campaigns, there remains a large gap between attitudes and behaviours.

Transplantation mythology flourishes as entertainment within popular culture where few positive or even accurate portrayals of the process are represented despite a hint of fact. These portrayals have a powerful effect upon audiences in their understanding of transplantation and in creating and reaffirming transplantation mythology. Transplantation myths function as 'story[s]-as-warning; an end in itself dispersed by widespread social distrust (Donovan 2002: 208) and are an example of what Reese (2001: 9) refers to as 'second-hand reality'. As such, the myths are formed by media exposure rather than being based on actual personal experience (which is rare) or from active research into authoritative information sites. Second-hand reality is significant in constructing public opinion and knowledge about organ donation and transplantation as the information can be framed in different ways, meaning that recipients can be predisposed 'toward a particular line of reasoning or outcome – with major behavioural consequences' (McCombs & Ghanem, 2001: 77). As a result, particular framings of transplantation in popular culture revolve around myths, narratives and metaphors that are well-understood and accepted by the public and, thus, create a fictionalised second-hand reality embedded into wider culture. This embedding is aided by entertainment media acting out scenes that add to the persuasive power of a message unlike news media (Morgan, Palmgreen, Stephenson, Hoyle & Lorch, 2003).

A recurring theme in transplantation myths within popular culture is that the dead donor, through the donated organs, continues to possess significant agency. This agency grants symbolic value and power by continuing the transmission of the continuance of transplantation mythology. Studies of television shows with organ transplantation storylines and their impact on viewers' attitudes, knowledge and behaviours regarding organ donation and transplantation consistently reveal negative representations (Morgan et al, 2009). The portrayal of the afterlife of transplanted organs and limbs from the dead within entertainment shows reflects deeply held real cultural concerns and anxieties bound up and explored within popular culture. These portrayals affirm existing transplantation myths that the process of donation is exploitative, transplants are conducted by corrupt doctors or leave the viewer imagining that a 'strange part may take over control' (Slatman and Widdershoven, 2010: 73) of the recipient. What is most notable about these transplantation myths within popular culture is that they would not spread and continue to exist unless people found the core ideas credible (Campion-Vincent, 2002). Therefore, to understand the miseducation of the public and the pervasive nature of the transplantation mythology, it is vital to consider the contribution of popular culture representations of organ donation and transplantation.

FOUR PROMINENT TRANSPLANTATION MYTHS

It is common to think of myths as the polar opposite of science and, therefore, lacking in significance in Western contemporary society, which relies so heavily on scientific understandings of the world. However, myths remain important even in the era of science. Myths lie at the heart of what is considered significant in individual lives and the world in which we live. Myths are not lies or detached stories. Myths 'are imaginative patterns, networks of powerful symbols that suggest particular ways of interpreting the world.' (Midgley, 2004: 1). Myths shape meaning and how society and individuals see themselves. They are not 'merely a surface dressing of isolated metaphors…[an] optional decorative paint' (Midgley, 2004: 3) but are integral to societal thinking and understanding. Mythology in contemporary times is a way in which we imagine the world and what is determined to be important within in it. The symbolism of mythology is key to the 'formation of official, literal, thoughts and descriptions' (Midgley, 2004: 3). With myths being infused with this symbolic power, they contain value for those who engage with them, none more so than those surrounding the dead and organ transplantation played out in popular culture.

Organ transplantation myths are explored within popular culture (limited here to television and film) from three broad categories: slasher-horror movies, where people are grievously injured and their bodies are restored; love stories where loved ones die and their organs are transplanted; and futuristic science fiction exploring the growing problem of organ shortages and creative ways of ensuring organs are available. A range of themes emerge in transplantation myths as recurring narrative tools in popular culture according to O'Neill's (2006) coherent chronological development of film representation of transplantation between the 1930s–2000s. In this chapter, these themes are consolidated and adapted to entail four prominent myths. Notably, the majority of the plots within transplantation stories reveal few positive or even accurate portrayals of the process within popular culture. However, with the popular culture purpose being to entertain rather than inform, it is perhaps unsurprising that the myths emerging within film and television portrayals are based on the worst urban legends and scenarios imaginable (O'Neill, 2006; Youngner, 1996; Squier, 2002). The influence of popular culture should not be underestimated, and such representations do lay a foundation of knowledge and perception that can adversely affect people's decision to donate (O'Neill, 2006: 222).

The first myth is the *threat of science*, whereby man plays God and the consequences are an affront to nature. This myth explores the idea of man, through science, being able to create life and suggesting human attempts to improve or replicate humans is an insult to Nature. This myth began to widely circulate from the 1930s and peaked between the 1950s–1960s where science is shown to be obsessed with creating life and doing the impossible. It reflects the idea of man as God. The threat to science myth in popular culture shares the same underlying message that any human attempt to improve on or even replicate humans is an act of unforgivable arrogance (van Riper, 2003). Nowhere is this more effectively portrayed than in fictional accounts of xenotransplantation where animal organs are transplanted into humans. Fiction reflects fact in contemporary times with the rise in pig and cow tissue being successfully used in some heart valve replacements. Some film representations of transplantation as the threat of science myth examines it through the potential damage to identity. The 1997 film *Face/Off* portrayed the frightening and negative impact that face transplantation can have on the lives of those involved by misusing identity as the face is an intrinsic and vital part of an individual's identity. The film highlighted the threat posed by science by exploring the ramifications of transplantation of visible organs such as the face.

The second myth is *misplaced trust*. This myth became distinctive within popular entertainment in the late 1960s focusing on the narrative of corruption in the medical system particularly regarding the procurement and allocation of organs. This myth maintains its potency with continuing organ shortages and reflected in films such as *Coma* (1978) where organs are being retrieved from comatose patients for transplant. The procurement of organs, including where they have come from and the manner by which they were procured and harvested, is a crucial component in the 'misplaced trust' myth. The myth often has a story resolution involving an ethical discussion between medics—a senior figure and a young idealistic doctor—ending with the senior figure being discredited or killed off and the young doctor left to carry on his or her ethical career. For organ donation and transplantation to work, the donation must be voluntary and bodies of potential donors—living and dead—are protected and not exploited by those charged with their care (Scheper-Hughes 2001, p. 59). This is undermined in popular culture with doctors often shown to be manipulating the organ allocation system to favour their patients or lying to hospital committee members about the eligibility of a patient for a transplant, thus placing their judgement over medical realities or fairness of organ allocation (Morgan, Movius, and Cody, 2009).

The myth of misplaced trust feeds into the third myth of *forced donation* relating to tales of organ theft and the black market for human organs. Anxieties and the ethics of acquiring organs within the fictional realm reflect wider societal concerns about organ donation, particularly due to the noted growth in the 21st century for black market organs (Ambagtsheer & Weimar, 2012). This is exemplified by fictional accounts of illicit or illegal procurement of organs including narratives of organ theft from individuals who are drugged and wake up discovering an organ, such as a kidney, has been removed. Such tales have a global range and have provoked resistance to presumed consent in respect of organ harvesting, concerns regarding attacks on foreigners and the trafficking of children's bodies and body parts as well as debate surrounding coerced gifts from prisoners in exchange for a reduction in prison sentence (Scheper-Hughes 2001: 32, 35). Organ transplantation within this myth is seen as exploitation involving illicit procurement, trade in organs from powerless donors, allocation of organs to the privileged fuelling fear that people will be killed for organs and even suggesting graverobbing (Youngner, 1996).

The fourth and final myth is *lack of control*. This is the most pervasive and broadest myth covering a variety of different themes, such as transplantation of limbs and internal organs possessing cellular memory (where the transplanted tissue exerts some degree of control or influence over the recipient). Dating from some of the earliest films made, stories of limbs transplantation from donors who have committed murder or rape are common. For example, *The Hands of Orlac* (1924) and in *Mad Love* (1935) where a pianist is given a hand transplant, not knowing the hands once belonged to a murderer. The hands exert control over the recipient leading to murderous consequences. Other threats to control are portrayed in futuristic science fiction representations of compulsory organ donation, xenotransplantation, eugenics, and even cloning. Cloning appears regularly in film including in *The Island* (2005) and *Never Let Me Go* (2010) where control is examined through the ethics of using human clones to solve organ shortages and the lack of control the clones have over their individuality and bodies. The fundamental value of the fourth myth and the previous three is that they would not spread and continue to exist unless people found the core ideas credible (Campion-Vincent, 2002). These accounts are connected to elements of truth in varying degrees and apparently validate cultural beliefs and fears about control over the body. At the heart of these myths is the reinforcement of concerns that social inequality will extend as far as the sanctity of individual bodies. The wealthy can buy the organs of the poor or the cloned, or they can demand them from the young. Underpinning the myth are superstitions and anxieties linked to fundamental concepts of control and tapping into a deep-rooted, culturally held terror of losing the ability to exert control over the self.

A fundamental theme within the losing control myth is loss of control as a direct result of the transplantation. This is the fear of losing control whereby organ recipients find their new body part exerts influence over them following a transplant. In a similar way to science fiction tales of human possession by aliens, who take over control (*Invaders from Mars*, 1953; *The Host*, 2013), transplant recipients are portrayed in the myth as vulnerable to losing control. This loss of control appears in two forms: firstly, via limb transplants that take over the recipients completely and physically control them; and, secondly, via organ transplants that lead to the repression and changing of the recipient's personality. This embodies cultural fears relating to body integrity and Western expectations and normalisation of individuality, autonomy and identity. Tales regarding the transplantation of limbs from donors who have committed murder or rape are common from the earliest films. Rooted in the history of corpse medicine where the criminal dead possessed mystic healing powers (Penfold-Mounce, 2010; Sugg, 2011), this alleged power of the dead body has been adapted and interwoven into transplant mythology of losing control. O'Neill (2006) identifies such loss of control via limb and brain transplants that have murderous result, for example in *The Hands of Orlac* (1924), *Mad Love* (1935), *The Brain That Wouldn't Die* (1962), *The Amazing Transplant* (1970) and in *Body Parts* (1991). Other transplant stories about losing control are embodied by films, such as *Mansion of the Doomed* (1976) and *The Eye* (2008), which both convey corneal transplants underpinned by the genre of horror. The popular representation of a solution to the loss of control is to 'amputate the organ, to somehow kill the rebellious body part' (O'Neill, 2006: 224).

What is notable in these tales of losing control is the dominant theme of the donor being criminal and the repeated portrayal of limbs transplantation rather than internal organs (although the brain transplant is an exception). There are no tales, for instance, of a liver donated by a criminal causing the organ recipient to become a murderer but many where a hand has been transplanted. Interestingly, this myth is so strong that popular culture does not just retell the myth but even pokes fun at it. *The Simpsons* have explored the losing control myth via a donated criminal body whereby Homer receives a hair transplant from the recurring criminal character, Snake. The transplanted hair controls Homer causing him to murder two of the witnesses to Snake's crime, and he barely avoids killing his son, Bart, before the hair is shot dead by Police Chief Wiggan[2]. Notions of organs or limbs retaining power to control or influence the recipient continue and have evolved beyond the idea of a battle for dominance between a limb transplant and the recipient. Instead, the myth of losing control is shifting towards subtler understandings of control.

The transplanted body part enacted by these myths lends life to something that becomes a bio-object on donation. As it moves between owners, the organ is a bio-object that challenges and disrupts cultural, social and institutional boundaries[3], and it does this by carrying with it mythical and symbolic values. The four myths that have been outlined all possess these values and emphasise the agency possessed by the dead. Being dead does not make the dead or their body parts inactive or unable to execute actions. Instead, each myth demonstrates how the dead continue to have agency in death. For example, the threat of science myth highlights how organ donation from the dead has been a catalyst to the debate surrounding science of how far is too far? When does science overstep the mark and play God? What should the boundaries be between life and death and what should not be crossed by scientific achievement? In this myth the dead have significant agency in stimulating consideration of boundary crossing. This is also the case in the misplaced trust myth and forced donation. Both of these myths focus on ethical dilemmas surrounding the use of organs from the dead (and admittedly also the living who are forced).

Through these myths, the agency of the dead brings to light the clear risks of not regulating limb and organ donation and the horrors of criminal exploitation, particularly of economic inequalities leading to forced donation. The final myth of losing control takes the agency of the dead further and in the most physical sense whereby the dead person's body part does not remain a bio-object but very distinctively takes the original owner's personality or soul with it into the recipient. This myth is just the starting point of even more complex debates surrounding controversial transplantation processes, such as animal-human hybrids, genetically modified organisms or transgenics. All these developments connect with the losing control myth (and the threat of science myth). They question and destabilise boundaries between human and animal, organic and nonorganic and living and the suspension of living (the meaning of death itself) and how identities are to be negotiated and stabilised. Organ transplantation and its four dominant myths mark the starting point for bio-objects to challenge conventional cultural, scientific, and institutional orderings and classifications (Holmberg, Schwennesen & Webster, 2011).

TRANSPLANTATION, BODILY CONTROL AND
CELLULAR MEMORY

In this next section, the problematizing of boundaries, identity and control raised by the fourth myth (losing control) will be explored in more detail. It is this myth that feeds most strongly into the argument of the agency of the dead for the loss of control by the organ or limb recipient due to the transplant highlights the ability of the dead to assert their influence over the living. Popular culture narratives reinforce cultural beliefs that body parts, such as limbs or organs, contain power or memory, which can be transferred to the donor after death (Penfold-Mounce, 2010). The dead maintain agency as a transplant that seeks to dominate and influence the recipient from beyond the grave and as a bio-object that disrupts widely accepted social and cultural boundaries between living and non-living, natural and artificial, etc. The losing control myth has evolved beyond the initial popular culture narratives of limb transplants taking over recipients at a physical level and controlling their movements and actions. Cellular memory is the next stage of the loss of control myth. This is where the dead have agency not just in extending the life of a recipient or even by taking them over but instead by causing mysterious behavioural symptoms and feelings of intense identification with donors. This is an afterlife for the dead not as a paranormal apparition but a second life within a transplant recipient body and over which a subtle control is asserted. The dead are able to be active from beyond the grave through their donated organs or limbs by influencing and changing the living.

Cellular memory is particularly bound up with the agency of the dead in being able to pass on emotions from the donor to the recipient. This is often explored as a form of loss of control through stories about love which focus on heart transplants. These tales repeatedly explore the idea of an organ being bound up with emotion, namely, the ability to love. For example, in *Untamed Heart* (1993), the lead character, Adam, turns down a heart transplant as he fears he will not love his girlfriend (Caroline) in the same way with a transplanted heart:

> Caroline: Adam, your heart is diseased! You need a new one.
>
> Adam: But this is my heart! I'm afraid that if they take it away, I won't be able to love you the same.
>
> Caroline: You love with your mind and your soul, not your heart.
>
> Adam: [touching his chest] Then how come I hurt here when you're not with me?

Other versions of cellular memory in transplanted hearts include loved ones dying and their heart being transplanted with the survivors falling in love with the transplant recipient or the organ recipient falling in love with the donor's partner (*Return to Me*, 2000; *A Stranger's Heart*, 2007).

Cellular memory as part of the loss of control myth gains a degree of credibility in two ways, both of which prevent it from being easily dismissed and reinforce the argument that the dead can exert agency, firstly, through its relationship with science and pseudo-science, and secondly through reported non-fictional cases. Cellular memory attains believability by being underpinned by elements of science and pseudo-science beyond popular culture portrayals (Pearsall, Schwartz and Russek, 1999). This makes it almost impossible to entirely refute and reflects persistent anomalous experiences by (a minority of) transplantation recipients following surgery. Cellular memory seeks to explain anomalous experiences of transplant recipients, experiences which are not supposed to be mechanically feasible for as the medical realm states: the transplant process is 'purely mechanical' (Le Breton, 1993: 290). Cellular memory theory from the 1970s is used to suggest that all living cells possess within them 'memory' and 'decider' functional subsystems (Miller, 1978) and dynamical energy systems theory proposed in the late 1990s (Schwartz & Russek, 1997; Schwartz and Russek, 1998). This provides logic for the concept that energy and information is stored to various degrees in cellular systems, and therefore, that memory can be present in these systems (Pearsall, Schwartz & Russek, 1999: 66). Therefore, the dead can pass on memory through transplanted organs as 'cellular memory' thereby explaining changes in transplant recipients that parallel the personality, identity or memory of the donor. Consequently, cellular memory makes it plausible that 'transplant patients may evidence personal changes that parallel the history of their donors' (Pearsall, Schwartz & Russek, 1999: 65) and that the dead maintain agency despite death.

Non-fictional accounts of anomalous experiences by transplant recipients also underpin the credibility of cellular memory. Popular culture representations contain a mixture of vague urban myth-like accounts and media reports of cellular memory experiences by organ recipients. This combination of urban myth and media reports support not only the argument of the agency of dead through their transplanted organ but are also presented as a form of evidence of the existence of cellular memory as a phenomenon outside of the fictional realm. Tales include cases of transplant recipients who claim that aspects of the donor's identity have been incorporated via the process of organ transplantation (Haddow, 2005). Cases range from a previously gay woman becoming straight after a heart transplant as well as developing a revulsion for meat, to another heart recipient who developed a love of classical music like his donor who was a keen violinist (Pears-all, Schwartz & Russek, 1999). Another urban myth-like example entails the instance of a child heart recipient with recurring nightmares of the murder of the donor that were so detailed the police were able to find and convict the murderer (Pearsall, Schwartz & Russek, 1999). Notably, the identity of this child is unknown. Some transplant victims have written about their experiences, such as Claire Sylvia who wrote *A Change of Heart* in 1997 about her experiences of receiving a new heart and lungs in 1988 in Connecticut in the United States. After the operation, she developed a love for green peppers, chicken nuggets and beer along with recurring dreams of 'Tim L'. Searching obituaries, she identified the heart donor and met the family, discovering her new tastes reflected Tim's in life (Sylvia, 1997). Sylvia may not have developed criminal tendencies or fallen in love with her donor's partner as portrayed in many films, but her case does suggest identity and personality shifts following a transplant.

Documented accounts of transplant recipients reporting cellular memory experiences whereby they develop behavioural symptoms and feelings of intense identification with their unknown donors (Lock, 2002) are a minority. These cases have varying degrees of verification, but when combined with the perceived credibility of science, they add currency to fictional accounts in popular culture (Morgan, Harrison, Long, Afifi, Stephenson, Reichert, 2005). As a result, cellular memory as an expression of agency by the dead to influence and even control the living retains a degree of validity. Furthermore, it feeds into cultural fears about transplant recipients never quite losing the 'otherness that derives from their [new organ] having belonged to another human being' (McKenny, 1999: 355). It also overrides scepticism and unanswered questions, such as if cellular memory exists why does it only affect a very small percentage of organ recipients? Popular representations of cellular memory have entered the collective consciousness and sow doubt that transplantation does not raise the possibility of loss of control by the organ recipient and pose a risk to bodily integrity.

Cellular memory is a specific form of narrative within the organ transplantation myth of losing control in which donated body parts from the dead are reported to exert agency. Whether cellular memory actually exists outside of urban myths or in documented cases is not under consideration here but the fact that these tales exist and perpetuate themselves highlights that the dead certainly have agency at this mythic level. Significantly, the agency of the dead means that it brings them into direct conflict with the agency of the living recipient. For the organ recipient, cellular memory is a potential threat to their agency in exerting their personality and character such as via taste in food and music or even their sexual orientation. Reports of cellular memory portray these changes as being intriguing and out of the ordinary or even funny. However, what is not considered is the potential emotional and mental trauma to the organ recipient at their perceived loss of control and agency over their body and sense of self. It is this conflict between the agency of the dead and agency of the living that lies at the heart of the losing control myth. For without the conflict between recipient and cellular memory, the losing control myth would be undermined and unable to exist.

CONCLUSION

Donation and transplantation of organs from the dead is an established and normalised, albeit specialist, area of medicine in the 21st century. It is consistently pushing at the boundaries of what medicine is capable of achieving, as professionals seek to transplant more complex components of the dead human body beyond internal organs to increasingly visible limb transplants such as hands and face transplants and even plans for the first head transplant[4]. However, transplantation is haunted by the continuing existence of myths dating back to before it was medically possible. Transplantation mythology highlights the agency of the dead as bio-objects that challenge social and cultural boundaries and explore the conflict that can ensue between organ or limb with the recipient. These myths are also bound up with the symbolic value of donated human body from the dead by providing an afterlife, which reinforces deeply held cultural beliefs and fears about the body and bodily integrity including ownership and identity, consent, social inequality and ethics. Like any myths, those surrounding transplantation are difficult to irrevocably refute, and they linger in contemporary times causing doubts and encouraging people to consider possibilities of the agency held by the dead. The dead, in bits, continue to engage the imagination and the possibility of an afterlife as well as the problems this poses for the living.

The significance of myths in relation to the dead is not only because they are compelling stories but also a network of powerful symbols for interpreting the world (Midgley, 2004). As such, the role of myth surrounding the use of organs and limbs from the dead should not be underestimated for they provide a way of projecting a type of agency onto and into the dead as bio-objects. Notably, mythology focused on the dead is not limited to transplantation but has a long and rich history in relation to the afterlife across the world. Myths grant a transgressive element to death and the dead allowing them agency and the power to influence and shape thoughts about mortality. Nowhere is this more evident than in cellular memory, which grants agency that is 'out of control' and bound up in the bio-object. This is acutely portrayed in the myths relating to the reanimation of the dead, not only via transplantation myths but also the living dead otherwise known as the Undead. The Undead are not limited by cultural boundaries or time and, as such, appear in varied forms of which the zombie and vampire are the most common. In the next chapter, the Undead, as a fictional reanimated corpse, are argued to be critical in enabling the individual as a consumer of popular culture to engage with fears and beliefs about mortality.

NOTES

1. Moran, L., (25 Sept 2014). Dutch Man turns amputated leg into a lamp, tried to sell it on ebay. *NY Daily News* http://www.nydailynews.com/news/world/man-turns-amputated-leg-lamp-sell-ebay-article-1.1952268 [accessed 15/2/2016]

2. *The Simpsons* (1998) Halloween 'Treehouse of Horror IX' Season 10.

3. Holmber, T. What are bio-objects? http://uu.diva-portal.org/smash/get/diva2:565076/FULLTEXT01.pdf [accessed 18/10/2017]

4. Brown, L. (20 Sept 2016) The surgeon who wants to perform a head transplant by 2017. *BBC News*. http://www.bbc.co.uk/newsbeat/article/37420905/the-surgeon-who-wants-to-perform-a-head-transplant-by-2017 [accessed 02/03/2017]

4

THE UNDEAD, MORBID SENSIBILITY AND MORBID SPACE

Although death may be muted in conversation and social life in Western culture, despite the emerging death positivity movement of the 21st century, it is vibrantly evident in popular culture. Nowhere is this vibrancy more clearly represented than in portrayals of the Undead. As an embodiment of death, the Undead are monstrous animated corpses that have captivated public fascination within popular culture for decades as well as in literature and myth long before that. The Undead appear in folktales from around the world and take varied forms ranging from incorporeal spirits, such as a banshee, ghost, poltergeist, or wraith to living (or reanimated) corpses, including the draugr, ghoul, revenent, mummy, jangshi, wight, vampire and zombie. New Undead beings have also continued to emerge within popular culture narratives such as the inferi in the Harry Potter series. The predominant type of Undead, that fall into the living corpse category in Western popular culture portrayals, are zombies and vampires. As such, they will be the focus of this chapter and the term Undead will be used forthwith to refer specifically and only to these two types of the Undead. Zombies in the context of this chapter will refer to people who have died and been reanimated and to the living who have become zombified via infection. The latter have not undergone physical death but have undergone death through a complete demise of self-awareness and selfhood. Zombies and vampires as the Undead encapsulate the ultimate abjection of the corpse; they are dead but reanimated, fearsome, and cannibalistic, but beyond that they have little in common regarding how they are portrayed. The Undead are polarised in their representation with zombies being similar to a plague, a threat to the living, something to be fought and resisted at all costs; in contrast, vampires are sexually desirable, charismatic and uniquely individual whilst embodying immortal youthful beauty. Despite these opposing representations of the Undead, both achieve massive popular culture appeal and, thus, are achieving agency as corpses that entertain and challenge social norms and anxieties relating to death and the dead.

Contemporary society has witnessed an explosion of the Undead in popular culture firmly establishing a 'gothic renaissance' where the cult of the dead is thriving (Khapaeva, 2017) and iterating how they are successful in entertaining on a mass scale. From even a cursory glance at viewing figures for television shows focused on the Undead, it is clear that the appeal is high. For example, the first season of *The Vampire Diaries* in 2006 attracted an average of 3.6 million viewers making it the most-watched series on the CW network until 2012. Meanwhile zombies have attracted an even larger audience of Undead enthusiasts with *The Walking Dead* attracting viewing figures of 17.1 million for the first episode of season seven in 2016. Although these figures dropped to under 11 million by the fifth episode, it continues to gather impressive audience numbers[1]. The visual consumption of the Undead as entertainment commands a significant global audience emphasising they should not be underestimated as an important and influential facet within contemporary culture. The popularity of the Undead have even arguably helped them achieve a state of idealization suggesting a radical rejection of human exceptionalism and leaving humanity not as an ultimate value but to be consigned to obsolescence (Khapaeva, 2017: 181). The Undead as entertainment in popular culture wield agency in a different way to those discussed in previous chapters. This chapter seeks to understand the agency of the Undead through two concepts: morbid sensibility and morbid space. It suggests the Undead are an embodiment of morbid sensibility and is, therefore, a vehicle for consumers of Undead popular culture narratives to consider death's relationship with the body and selfhood within morbid space.

THE UNDEAD AND MORBID SENSIBILITY

The Undead are a potent and common form of entertaining corpse within popular culture, appearing in comic books, television shows, video games and films. They have even inspired Undead fan engagement via an abundance of vampire online fan sites and even zombie walks[2] where participants indulge in their love of dressing up as brain-eating reanimated corpses. The popularity and the appeal of the Undead, who are reanimated corpses with monstrous tendencies, needs little reconsideration as many scholars from a variety of disciplinary backgrounds have already led the way on this issue (Egginton, 2016; Hubner, Leaning & Manning, 2014; Platts, 2013). Therefore, the key questions here are what is the Undead relationship with morbid sensibility and what is the significance of this relationship? Please note that morbidity in the context of this research is used to refer to public fascination with the morbid, macabre, death and corpses rather than 'sickness'. As such, the concept of morbid sensibility is used to illustrate how individuals and society become open to deliberating mortality within popular culture. This is particularly evident in the consumption of the horror/fantasy genre where the Undead exist. It is the rich vein of popular culture portrayals of the Undead that highlight how a societally sensitive topic can become part of everyday conversation and even be consumed as entertainment (Penfold-Mounce, 2015). Consequently, morbid sensibility refers to people's willingness to deliberate death in the context of popular culture and that the Undead are a key embodiment of this morbid sensibility. Through the Undead as an incarnation of morbid sensibility, people who consume this form of popular culture are able to explore what public wisdom commonly asserts is taboo. They encourage the viewer's morbid sensibility to consider the prospect that ultimately all of humanity will eventually rot and decay without thought or control. As Walters (2004) notes, this prospect, and related fear, fascinates people and is a key appeal of horror where the viewer is able to look at what is normally avoided allowing for a cathartic purging of fear. Consequently, morbid sensibility is a vehicle for people to respond to and deliberate death and the dead without concern of being censured or criticised for being overly macabre or morbid. Therefore, the Undead matter as a cultural object as their agency is rooted in stimulating and enabling viewers' imagination about death and mortality as well as wider issues about social life, values and ideologies (Platts, 2013).

The Undead demonstrate considerable agency via the morbid sensibility of the consumer. They enable individuals who consume such tales to develop an advanced sociological imagination (Mills, 1959) which engages with not only key sociological themes, such as gender and sexuality, health and illness and class but also to wrestle with such issues using death and the dead as a conduit. Morbid sensibility adds in issues of mortality to the sociological imagination where 'people make their own history but under circumstances of their own choosing' (Beer & Burrows, 2010: 235). Thus, 'the lived relationship between public issues and private troubles; and the interminable struggle between human agency and social structures' (Beer & Burrows, 2010: 235) are encouraged and explored by non-sociologists through vehicle of the Undead as morbid sensibility. The Undead have significant agency and influence upon consumers because

> one can even 'know' about them [...] without actually reading vampire fiction or watching vampire films. In this sense, they are 'in' culture; and they may well have (or be mobilised to have) 'real' effects. (Gelder, 1994: x).

By consuming the Undead, viewers experience the effects Gelder (1994) highlights, as they are able to explore central sociological debates without being fully aware of what they are doing, resulting in individuals unwittingly becoming sociologists and death scholars. Consequently, the Undead are a vital form of 'social-science fiction', a concept that refers to something that inspires the sociological imagination of the scholar and non-scholar alike but is fiction (Penfold-Mounce, Beer & Burrows, 2011; Reed & Penfold-Mounce, 2015). As social-science fiction the Undead reflects the value of using popular culture as a data source within social-science research for 'to say that the zombie [or vampire] is fictional is not to say that it does not comment on the real' (Muntean & Payne, 2009: 245). In fact, the Undead, despite being firmly rooted in the horror/fantasy genre, are effective in reflecting and reproducing aspects of the real social world.

Popular culture narratives about the Undead as social-science fiction are particularly valuable due to their state of constant flux and development. The Undead keep evolving and demonstrate agency through this continual renewal and change that prevents either zombies or vampires from being typecast as a particular type of reanimated corpse. Importantly, although the Undead continue to change and develop, they still maintain an enduring and recurring recognisable cultural motif. They remain at their core a conventional monster, something other than human and, therefore, monstrous and fear-inducing. Changes in how the Undead are portrayed has led to a plethora of differences emerging, not only between zombies and vampires as different types of the Undead but also differences within these two types. This highlights a distinct lack of equality between zombies and vampires and how they embody morbid sensibility differently for, although both are reanimated corpses, they 'engage audiences differently: the zombie incites fear, while the sympathetic vampire incites desire' (Tenga & Zimmerman, 2013: 77). This ability for variance between and within Undead types allows a flexibility for how morbid sensibility is engaged and used by viewers to explore different issues and ideas.

Zombies as vehicle for morbid sensibility have undergone significant change since their early portrayals in popular culture, so much so that different zombie representations often struggle to share commonalities. This is particularly the case since entering a 'zombie renaissance' in the early 21st century (Hubner, Leaning & Manning, 2014). Zombies are still predominantly decaying, mindless, often brain-eating reanimated corpses (*Night of the Living Dead*, 1968; *Dawn of the Dead*, 1978, *Day of the Dead*, 1985; *The Walking Dead,* 2010–present) but who are sometimes scarily fast (*28 Days Later,* 2002; *28 Weeks Later*, 2007) as opposed to moving with traditional shuffling steps. Some zombie portrayals have shifted from the horror genre into comedy, such as *Fido* (2006), *Shaun of the Dead* (2004) and *Zombieland* (2009) as well as entering the horror-drama and science fiction thriller genres where science explains the Undead. This is effectively illustrated in *In the Flesh* (2013–2014) where zombies are identified as sufferers of 'partially deceased syndrome' and treated with medication for this illness. Meanwhile, in *World War Z* (2013), the zombie condition is portrayed as a highly contagious plague but the immune are those who have suffered or are suffering from serious illness. The evolution of the zombie continues beyond these instances to even include them being able to regain their humanity, endure guilt and become a romantic lead (*Warm Bodies*, 2013), to appear in a historical drama (*Pride and Prejudice and Zombies*, 2016) or to be able to supress zombie tendencies by eating corpse brains from a mortuary and develop crime-solving capabilities (*IZombie*, 2015–present). These different and varied incarnations of the zombie reveal it as a highly versatile type of the Undead providing a vehicle for morbid sensibility that is flexible and fertile. Through the zombie, the viewer's morbid sensibility can explore issues ranging from (but not limited to) fears over loss of control over the body and selfhood (similar to the loss of control myth examined in Chapter 3) to fear of death and decay and from cannibalism to a collapse of society and governance and even to family and kinship ties. The zombie is a quintessential vehicle for morbid sensibility.

Vampires, in contrast to their Undead cousin the zombie, have evolved less dramatically and are, therefore, a less versatile tool for morbid sensibility. The main change for vampires has been a shift from being only portrayed as monstrous, ruthless predators (*Dracula*, 1931; *From Dusk till Dawn*, 1996) to include a tangential vampire types who are sympathetic, sexually desirable blood drinkers (*Twilight Saga*, 2008-2012; *True Blood*, 2008-2014) and even some comic portrayals

(*Abbott and Costello Meet Frankenstein*, 1948; *The Fearless Vampire Killers*, 1967; *My Best Friend Is a Vampire*, 1988; and *Dracula: Dead and Loving it*, 1995). Morbid sensibility through vampires is inextricably interwoven with the long and well-established history of sexual desirability for, in contrast to the zombie, they lack 'the reality of a corpse: they are pristine, perfectly preserved, and sexually potent.' (Tenga & Zimmerman, 2013: 78). Vampires are erotic creatures conflating sex and death and this combination has directed the agency of vampires as morbid sensibility towards exploring gender and sexuality. From their earliest literary origins, such as *Carmilla* (1871–1872) where a young woman is preyed upon by a female vampire, vampires have embraced marginalised ideals and consistently challenge social constructs and contemporary notions of gender and sexuality (Vincent, 2015). Films, such as *Blood and Roses* (1960) *The Karnstein Trilogy* (1970–1971) and *Vampyres* (1974), all explore lesbianism, whilst *Interview with the Vampire* (1994) showcases the suggestive relationship between Louis and Lestat, which focuses on the erotic attraction to the vampire rather than fear (Beck, 2011). Although vampires may lack significant new developments in contrast to the zombie, this does not hamper their value as an embodiment of morbid sensibility.

The traditional vampiric ability to embody subverted cultural norms, of repressed sexuality, the heteronormative and the gender binary that dictates traditional male and female roles (Vincent, 2015) remain hugely pertinent across time and cultures. They have the agency to embody polarised positions whereby they assert marginalised ideals and reassert patriarchy, racial superiority, nuclear family values, the traditional role of women in that family and chaste heterosexuality (Williamson, 2005; Silver, 2010). The massive international success of the *Twilight Saga* (2008–2012) is particularly illustrative of how patriarchal and nuclear family values can be asserted by vampires, firstly, through the representation of motherhood, which becomes a source of power that is not experienced by single women but which enables Bella, the lead protagonist of the story, to become a self-sacrificing warrior mother which grants her pleasure, satisfaction and authority. As such, the model of male/female relationships continues to reflect past traditional understandings of identity, gender and sexuality rather than offer a challenge. Secondly, it is the sexual relationship or rather abstinence of the two main protagonists, Bella and Edward (the lead vampire protagonist), which fails to challenge traditional roles and values. For as Edward exerts self-control over his blood lust he consistently refuses Bella's pursuit of sexual contact outside of marriage (Silver, 2010). Vampires, whether they subvert social norms or reinforce them, provide a key vehicle for their morbid sensibilities to examine death, gender and sexuality. Through the Undead, morbid sensibility has an ideal vehicle to allow people to deliberate fears around death and the dead and ultimately how 'death infect[s] life' (Kristeva, 1982: 4).

THE UNDEAD AND MORBID SPACE

As reanimated corpses that are consumed as entertainment, the Undead allow morbid sensibility to be indulged by viewers, but significantly they allow for, and inspire, very different engagements with shared social and cultural anxieties. In the second half of this chapter, the relationship that morbid sensibility shares with morbid space (Penfold-Mounce, 2015) will be explored. The Undead create and exist within morbid space, and it is this morbid space which provides a habitation for morbid sensibility to be stimulated within viewers. Morbid space refers to a conceptualisation of space and how it is moved through, lived within and consumed; it is about boundaries surrounding mortality and how these can be crossed or reinforced. It exemplifies how corpses and death are far from taboo but are instead ordinary and normalised whilst also becoming popularised, eroticised and even at times celebrated alongside societal ambivalence (Penfold-Mounce, 2015: 11). Until now, morbid space has only been used in relation to crime drama (Penfold-Mounce, 2015); however, it is equally useful when applied to the horror-fantasy setting of the Undead, which is fantastical, horrific and credible. The Undead appear in morbid environments, such as a post-apocalyptic world that has been overwhelmed, or is in the process of being overwhelmed, by the reanimated dead or a time and place where they live out an existence in hiding from the living. Many of these tales involve a pursuit for a cure, survival in a changed world or how to make a relationship work between the Undead and the living. Consumers of the Undead unlock morbid sensibility within morbid space where possibilities are explored whilst being entertained. In the remainder of this chapter, it will be argued that the Undead as an embodiment of morbid sensibility exist within morbid space and are a catalyst for the formation of two particular types of morbid space: 'safe' and 'provocative'. The following two sections within the chapter will consider how morbid sensibility through the vehicle of the Undead engages with questions about firstly the body and safe morbid space and, secondly, selfhood and provocative space.

The Body and Safe Morbid Space

The intellectual significance of the body within social science and humanities and how it accounts for embodies preconditions of agency and the physical effects of social structures is of enormous influence. The body has come to be recognised as thinking and feeling rather than disembodied minds unaffected by senses and habits (Schilling, 2004). The body remains increasingly difficult to define for, although the body may appear to be solid, it is 'the most elusive, illusory... metaphorical... and ever distant thing' (Turner, 1984: 8). Schilling's framework of interests that have driven the growth of body studies outline five sets of interests. Firstly, the analysis of consumer culture that has driven interest in the way bodies are consumed. Secondly, a concern with bodies in what he describes as 'second wave feminism'. Thirdly, Foucualdian work on governmentality and body control. Fourthly, the concern with technological developments and their implication for bodily reality. And finally, the interest in grounding conceptual ideas through the body as a focus point where the body is used as a conceptual resource. Schilling (2004) summarises these interests, saying

> These five strands of social thought/analytical concerns have done much to stimulate and maintain ah the rise of interest in the body since the 1980s, but they approached and defined the subject in very different ways. The body was a surface phenomenon which had become a malleable marker of commercial value subject to the vagaries of fashion for the theorists of consumer culture. It was a sexed object that had been used as a means of justifying women's sub-ordination for feminists. It was an object that had been rendered passive by changing modes of control for Foucauldian analysts of governmentality. The body was changed into an uncertain and even rapidly disappearing remnant of pre-technological culture for those interested in the meeting of meat and machines which had occurred with the development of cyborgs. Finally, it became

a positive conceptual category for those concerned
with addressing theoretical problems in their own
discipline.

Consequently, the body can and should be seen 'as a multi-
dimensional medium for the constitution of society' (2004: 9)
and, for the purposes of this chapter and its consideration of
the agency of the Undead body, the first and fifth sets of interests are particularly pertinent.

The consumption of the Undead by viewers, who are firmly rooted in the consumer culture, grants zombies and vampires a powerful agency as a vehicle for morbid sensibility.
Notably, the Undead do not exist in a vacuum but within a
predominantly horror/fantasy defined morbid space, which is
the spatial context in which morbid sensibility is explored by
the consumer. The Undead as morbid sensibility create and
define the formation of a particular type of morbid space,
which is referred to here as a 'safe morbid space'. This type of
morbid space provides a 'safe' place to openly consider and
consume gore and violence, death and the dead all of which
is, according to public wisdom, either a taboo or at least an
uncomfortable topic to discuss or individually contemplate.
The Undead in a safe morbid space provide a spatial context
where entertainment and deliberating death and the dead is
acceptable and even celebrated. The combination of a fictional but credible morbid space that is imaginative and specula-
tive creates safety from direct personal consequences (other
than viewers being made to jump and the odd bad dream). A
safe morbid space is, therefore, a shelter for consumers where
realism is suspended and, by embracing the Undead, they can
engage morbid sensibility.

In safe morbid space, the Undead display agency as they
render visible social norms, threats and anxieties about death
that underpin contemporary Western ways of thinking,

particularly about the body. Zombies for example, whilst being entertaining, suggest a fundamental shift in the perception of what is considered a threat to Western human subjectivity highlighted by a change from the slow shuffling zombies of the 1970s to being fast and lethal in films such as *28 Days Later* (2002). Changing depictions of zombies were effectively illustrated by transitioning depictions of zombies to become portrayed as a particular kind of threat following the 9/11 terrorist attack in the United States (Muntean & Payne, 2009). Zombies shifted from being merely a plague about to burst across society to initially living hidden within the midst of Western society, which is consequently vulnerable to death and violence. Consequently, the Undead are an insightful social text as they are a 'monstrous body… [of] pure culture' (Cohen, 1996: 4) who 'enact[…] a host of anxieties and desires, shifting shape as the culture they are brought to life in itself changes form' (George & Hughes, 2013: 1). The Undead have long been associated with notions of the monster and the monstrous, and this is particularly prevalent through the body. As the reanimated dead zombies and vampires offer a direct challenge to the boundary of life and death of the body as although they are dead, they are 'alive'. It is their status as challengers of the boundary between death and life that reinforce the agency of the Undead, making them into potentially revolutionary beings, capable of destabilising widely accepted social and cultural norms. Cohen (1996: 20) argues that the Undead's agency makes them particularly sociologically useful as they

> ask us how we perceive the world […] They ask
> us to re-evaluate our assumptions about race,
> gender, sexuality, our perception of difference, our
> tolerance toward its expression. They ask us why
> we have created them.

The Undead are effective in their ability to empower the audience to ask questions which are inherently sociological. Crucially, the audience is positioned in safe morbid space where the Undead and the bodies upon which they feed become a monstrous entertaining fairy tale separate from a narrative of realism.

Zombies in particular display agency as a threat to the boundaries surrounding the body of the human subject. The majority of popular culture portrayals consolidate the Western conception of zombies that differs significantly from African and Caribbean diaspora legends and stories that are interwoven with voodooism and voodoo magic (Davis, 2000; Ciekawy and Geschiere, 1998). Western zombies are literally a living death in that they are neither fully dead nor fully alive; they are dead bodies that are reanimated in that they are capable of moving about. Thus, zombies pose a threat by resisting the norms of the dead body, i.e., that corpses are lifeless and inanimate. The representation of the zombie body is dominated by them being damaged and decaying, clearly demarcating that they are not alive but reanimated corpses. *The Walking Dead* (2010–2017) pays attention to this trend by showing zombies attaining more advanced degrees of decomposition as the show progresses, highlighting the passage of time[3]. Consequently, zombies are a graphic reminder of mortality as they remain corpse-like and lack sentience, which is a contrast to the physical wholeness, individuality and desirability maintained by their Undead cousin the vampire. Zombies (as well as vampires) also pose a challenge to perceptions of the dead body by confronting viewers in social spaces where death is never visible (Austin, 2015). For example, the Undead do not stay confined to graveyards and crypts; they invade cities, homes and the landscape. They fragment boundaries between life and death making both categories meaningless, for the value that is placed on life is understood socially in terms of not being dead. If death is no longer death, but a kind of living death, namely a corpse that is reanimated, then death becomes a liminal space where boundaries are flexible and permeable rather than permanent (Lauro & Embry, 2008). In a safe morbid space, the Undead as morbid sensibility is able to explore where the boundary lies between the dead and the living, offering new insights to debates about the body.

As fictional monsters the Undead do more than just challenge boundaries surrounding the body via death and mortality but through the body as food. To the Undead, the human body is prey or rather a food source, with zombies traditionally targeting the human brain, whilst vampires are focused on human blood. These cannibalistic tendencies call into question the basic food taboo surrounding people as food whilst also reinforcing the deep-seated inequality between zombies and vampires as Undead monsters. Undead monsters have a hierarchy, and this is reflected in their consumption of different parts of the human body and how they actually eat. Vampires get to feed exclusively on human blood and this is often achieved via a sexual encounter although in *True Blood* (2008–2014) a synthetic blood is available. Meanwhile, zombies actively target humans and messily feast on their flesh and organs although some zombie protagonists such as Liv Moore in *IZombie* (2015-) will prepare human brains and eat them with delicacy and relish as part of a meal. However, a human is eaten; the Undead construct human bodies as consumables. They suggest the blurring of boundaries regarding the body as eatable and challenge the Western social norm of human beings being constructed as non-edible. The consumption of human flesh has been a long-held and deeply held social taboo in Western nations with cases of cannibalism stimulating particular disgust and concern. By disrupting the division between consumable and non-consumable flesh, the

Undead within safe morbid space are a tool through which to consider the question of why and how it is justifiable and societally acceptable for humans to consume the flesh of other animals (Bilewicz, Imhoff & Drogosz, 2011), but humans themselves cannot be consumed. The Undead threaten the sanctity of the human body both in being the *living* dead and by physically preying on the living.

The Undead body also plays a critical role through its embodiment of morbid sensibility and within a safe morbid space to engage sociological ideas of Otherness. The Undead are used to represent various kinds of Other, all of whom are outside social norms and considered monstrous and deviant non-subjects. This identity of Otherness is often depicted as a social threat and has included gender, sexuality and illness such as AIDS (Fink, 2010), class relations (Weed, 2009) and even schizophrenia and teen suicide (Kayton, 1972). However, the preeminent Othered identity embodied by the Undead is as monsters who are the abject Other for they are 'difference made flesh, come to dwell among us. In its function as dialectical Other… the monster is an incorporation of the Outside, the Beyond… but originate Within' (Cohen, 1996: 7). They are a perfect vehicle to consider Other as they are trapped in a liminal space, dead but still animate. The Undead monster exists beyond social norms created by various boundaries and represents a permanent threat. It forces people to question and reflect upon the social and cultural context that creates particular kinds of monsters and to consider why it is that they are considered threatening. Therefore, as monsters, the Undead linger around the margins of mortality, making them a useful 'metaphorical figure for the representation of otherness' (Campbell, 2013: 100). It has been argued that 'no other monster has endured, and proliferated, in quite the same way—or been made to bear such a weight of metaphor as the vampire' (Punter & Byron, 2004: 268), but a decade and more beyond this claim, it is evident that the zombie is coming to rival if not replace its Undead cousin as a preeminent social metaphor. The Undead exist within a safe morbid space for the viewer, who can vicariously experience death and the dead without having to actually physically contend with vampires or zombies. The Undead are only a physical threat to the characters within popular culture and not the audience. Consequently, they are a crucial tool for mobilizing morbid sensibility in this safe morbid space as they enable the scrutiny, consideration and speculation of social boundary crossing in relation to death and the body. Significantly, a safe morbid space is not the only type of morbid space the Undead create and exist within, for they also develop a 'provocative morbid space'.

Selfhood and Provocative Morbid Space

The Undead as an embodiment of morbid sensibility provide more than an entertaining and safe morbid space but also a 'provocative morbid space'. In this second type of morbid space, the Undead go beyond providing just a safe space without consequences to consider morbid sensibilities. Instead, the Undead in provocative morbid space succeed in provoking consumers to consider uncomfortable issues that might be avoided elsewhere, such as selfhood and loss of that selfhood. Loss of the sense of self is perceived as a fate worse than death and is consistently grappled with by the Undead. To be Undead is to be trapped in a body that has lost the essence of who the person was in life. It is to become monstrous through a collapse in sense of selfhood. It has been claimed that the vampire and zombie share a common characteristic in that they share the absence of some metaphysical quality of their essential selves' (Boon, 2011: 7). Zombies and vampires may lose an element of selfhood on becoming the Undead, but they experience this unequally and, as a result, create a provocative morbid space which forces morbid sensibility to contemplate different ways to consider selfhood and loss of selfhood.

Loss of selfhood is portrayed as far more complete in the case of zombies in Western popular culture than vampires and is typically traced back to George Romero's films in the late 1960s and 1970s: *Night of the Living Dead* and *Dawn of the Dead*. Romero's films set up a virtually unshakeable vision of zombies as animated corpses systematically lacking an essential feature of themselves making them effectively mindless with no free will. They are effectively bodies without minds and, as such, threaten Western understandings of what makes us individual subjects, namely a body controlled by its separate, rational, conscious mind. Moreover, rather than being individuals, they are part of a seething mass driven only by bodily desire to consume others. Emerging from the witchcraft beliefs and voodoo of West Africa and Haiti where a corpse can be reanimated and even controlled by a sorcerer, the zombie has evolved to become associated with infection, epidemics and contagion that create zones of 'ravenous flesh-eating dead' (Conrich, 2014: 16). This loss of selfhood is further reflected by the majority of zombies lacking dialogue, distinctive personalities or individualism and being portrayed as a direct threat to social order and making them into harbingers of chaos, anarchy and suffering. Consequently, the zombie becomes the exemplar Undead experiencing loss of selfhood.

In contrast to zombies who are largely defined by a loss of selfhood, vampires do not lose their sense of self and individuality. Admittedly, they are forced to grapple with monstrous desires, i.e., blood lust, but they are able to retain a degree of humanity and individual personalities. This retention of individualism and a form of selfhood is illustrated by the position vampires achieve within the majority of narratives in which they appear. The modern vampire is predominantly the protagonist and narrator and his or her feelings and emotions are central to the story (Khapaeva, 2017), such as in *Interview with a Vampire* (1994) where vampire Louis, an unwilling convert to the Undead, tells his tale to a journalist. Or, more often, the vampire shares key protagonist status with humans, such as in the *Twilight Saga*, where Bella Swan enters a relationship with the vampire Edward Cullen, or in *The Vampire Diaries* where Elena Gilbert is caught in a love triangle with vampire brothers Stephan and Damon Salvatore. Vampires are consistently central to the narrative plot aided by being elegant, embodying physical perfection whilst also being intelligent, with special gifts that surpass humans in every way. Vampires 'incarnate the nonhuman ideal of our times' (Khapaeva, 2017: 94) embodying everything the zombie is not. They encapsulate the contemporary focus on the pursuit of individualism, personhood, or individual rights. They are articulate, conservative and uphold social codes. What they most notably are not, is an embodiment of loss of self in an era where individualism and personhood is central to social norms.

Significantly, there are contemporary challenges to the dominance of vampires as individuals with a sense of selfhood with some zombies taking central character roles, such as in *IZombie* (2015–present), *Warm Bodies* (2003) and *The Returned* (2015), based on the French television series (2012; 2015) and film (2004), both named *Les Revenants*. However, in all these examples where zombies are the key protagonists, they grapple consistently with the threat of losing their individuality and semblance of selfhood, which is similar to the vampiric battle with blood lust. In *IZombie*, the zombie heroine Liv has to eat human brains in order to retain her selfhood whilst enduring personality traits of the brain donor personality or become a mindless, shuffling brain hungry zombie similar to those in Romero movies. Meanwhile, R in *Warm Bodies* regains his selfhood by eating the brain of the boyfriend of the girl that he then falls in love with, whereas *The Returned* tackles selfhood and identity from a different angle. In this case, the zombies are not compulsive monsters feeding on the human population but rather grappling with how the world and their loved ones have moved on since their death. Despite these examples, predominantly the zombie lacks a central character role other than as part of a horde. So, the contemporary Undead are divided in their experience, or retention, of their sense of self after death. As a result, zombies and vampires as an embodiment of moral sensibility stimulate a provocative morbid space where they are a catalyst for exploring fears and anxiety over not only death but also threats to selfhood.

According to Behuniak (2011), a provocative morbid space, where the Undead grapple with selfhood, can have wider implications and be linked to broader experiences of inequality. Behuniak (2011) argues that the zombie, and the portrayal of difference in the body of horrific Others, reinforces social inequalities. The zombies and their traditional lack of selfhood as a text does not simply offer a mirror to the social world but constructs it with negative real-world effects. This is especially evident in the zombie which has been explicitly imported into scholarly and popular representations of patients with Alzheimer's disease. As a result, we are witnessing that

> the frightening celluloid images of fictional
> characters called zombies have leaked into the
> popular and scholarly discourse about real people
> who have Alzheimer's disease, constructing them as
> animated corpses and their disease as a terrifying

threat to the social order. [...] The zombie instils
fear by drawing from cultural anxieties, and then
reflecting them back to the population that in turn
breaths life and strength into them by applying
this fictional representation to social realities.
(Behuniak, 2011: 72)

Zombie metaphors used in relation to Alzheimer's disease
include Alzheimer sufferers' physical appearance and their
loss of the self as the illness destroys the brain making it a literal living death. The disease is also described as an epidemic
that is ravaging an ageing population, placing an intolerable
burden on the young and the healthy. Behuniak (2011) links
this use of the zombie as a metaphor for Alzheimer's patients
to the formation of not only stigma but also evoking disgust.
The result being that those who suffer from this disease enter
into the category of being a monstrous Other who are a burden upon society, as opposed to a group of human beings
worthy of support and respect. Behuniak (2011) effectively
highlights how the Undead can become a social mechanism
which is detrimental to particular groups chiefly through a
loss of selfhood.

Zombies, as a critical vehicle for morbid sensibility, extend
beyond the average consumer to professional sociologists.
The zombie 'blankness' and lack of selfhood allow them to be
a workable vehicle for different sociological concerns meaning they can be used to theorise sociological trends and disasters. As Russell (2005: 23) claims, in 1930s America

The zombie and the stock market crash segued
neatly together, expressing the powerlessness that
so many felt as they suffered under an unstable
economy that reduced princes to paupers, bank
managers to bums.... The zombie, a dead worker

        resurrected as a slave into a hellish afterlife of
        endless toil was the perfect monster for the age.

This ability to represent a threat to social norms of human subjectivity is a crucial illustration of the value of zombies' loss of selfhood within provocative morbid space and reflects the socio-historical context in which they are portrayed. One classic zombie film, Romero's 1978 film *Dawn of the Dead*, has been subjected to in-depth analysis of its portrayal of the relationships between humans and zombies. As a group of survivors of the zombie apocalypse take refuge in a shopping mall surrounded by zombies, the film has been argued to be a satire of the emerging audience capitalism in the 1970s. Here the zombie genre is used to suggest how capitalist society has produced mindless, endless and destructive consumption causing no clear difference between the reanimated corpses and the human survivors (Jones, 2002, p. 163). This theme of a lack of selfhood and individualism is only reiterated, according to Pifer (2011), in *Shaun of the Dead* (2004), which offers a critique of working conditions under late capitalism where zombies are often undistinguishable and unnoticeable in relation to the human workers.

The hailed renaissance of the zombie by Hubner, Leaning and Manning (2014) can be extended to include the vampire. The contemporary Undead are changing from their historical origins as monstrous, terrifying creatures whose lust for human blood (vampires) or human brains (zombies) was destructive and dangerous. Today, the Undead have expanded beyond this monstrous Other that has lost their sense of selfhood and borne witness to the rise of a range of increasingly sympathetic creatures both zombie and vampire. The sympathetic Undead try to contain their monstrosity, feel guilt for their monstrous urges and often become desirable to humans. It would seem that the next stage of Undead is about vampires and zombies possessing selfhood and them grappling with guilt via their conscience. The Undead are shifting towards wrestling with their monster status and fighting to regain their humanity along with a sense of selfhood and individuality. It would seem that in the 21st century both the sympathetic zombie and 'vampire rule.... [meaning that] ... Little remains of Stoker's monstrous Count or the bestial bloodsuckers of East European folklore.' (George & Hughes, 2013: 5), but a new generation of the Undead pursuing selfhood is being born within, and because of, a provocative morbid space.

CONCLUSION

The Undead have significant agency despite being a fictional reanimated corpse. They are a vibrant form of social-science fiction that is internationally consumed as entertainment. The Undead are effective at entertaining viewers by thrilling, scaring, intriguing and revolting; they are convincingly credible and yet unreal. Through the Undead, people are able to consume death and the horrors of reanimation where notably becoming a vampire is far more desirable than a zombie. In this chapter, the agency of the Undead has been explored by using two concepts: morbid sensibility and morbid space. Through the first concept, it has been argued that the Undead not only expose the viewer to death and the dead in graphic visual detail, but they also embody morbid sensibility. The Undead mobilise morbid sensibility unlocking a candid state of mind and emotion about death and the dead. Zombies and vampires provoke a particular morbid sensibility and are a vehicle within the confines of the second concept of morbid space to examine sociological themes. In the two types of morbid space, safe and provocative, created by the Undead, people are able to mobilise morbid sensibility to explore social issues and fears ranging from the boundaries of death and life, to cultural norms about food and from disease perception to terrorist threats to governance and national security. The Undead as morbid sensibility and within the confines of morbid space, safe and provocative, inspires and challenges the audience to engage with shared fears relating to the body and selfhood alongside concerns about death. The next chapter moves away from the Undead in order to consider 'the authentic dead' and their role in challenging perceptions of the public wisdom that death is taboo.

NOTES

1. Jones, D. (28/11/2016) Viewing figures for Season Seven of *The Walking Dead* plummet. http://www.nme.com/news/music/viewing-figures-season-seven-walking-dead-plummet-1878325 [accessed 19/5/2017]

2. A zombie walk is an organised public gathering of people who dress up in zombie costumes. Originating in the 2000s, zombie walks are largely held in urban centres where the participants walk en masse around city stress and public spaces in an orderly fashion.

3. Eames, T. (2017, 7 November) See how *The Walking Dead's* zombies have gradually decayed over eight seasons. *Digital Spy*. http://www.digitalspy.com/tv/ustv/feature/g24608/walking-dead-zombies-walkers-decay-over-time-seasons-1-to-7/ [accessed 10/4/2018]

4. Carmilla is a Gothic novella written by Joseph Sheridan Le Fanu, which was serialised and published in the literary magazine *The Dark Blue* in late 1871 and early 1872.

5

CONFRONTING DEATH AND THE AUTHENTIC DEAD

We are living in a death denial society in which death is taboo. Or are we? Influential publications such as Jessica Mitford's *The American Way of Death* (1963) and Ernest Becker's *The Denial of Death* (1973) have contributed to the emergence of popular wisdom, which asserts that death is repressed, and it terrifies humans in the industrialised Western world. In light of this widely held belief in death taboo and death denial, death appears to be far from a go-to topic of conversation. It suggests that the West has 'fallen out of practice when it comes to the "everydayness" of death and dead bodies'[1] with cultural norms dictating that dead bodies should not be viewable outside of the funeral industry (Auchter, 2017: 223). Subsequently, these cultural taboos tell us that dead bodies do not belong in the public sphere and something extraordinary must be the case for them to be on display and rendered visible. Clearly, the West is ambivalent about the corpse, particularly regarding how it is displayed or hidden, revered or defiled, viewed as useful or waste, or as a source of entertainment or sombreness (Foltyn, 2008a). People are attracted to and repelled by death and the dead. However, despite the continuing debates and perceptions of death denial and death as taboo, the dead as an embodiment of death have never been more visually prominent and widely consumed in contemporary mass-mediated global society. The dead have never been more active with a plethora of the dead appearing in the news media and popular culture in graphic and intimate detail. The portrayal of the dead ranges from actual corpses in areas experiencing war or natural disasters to victims of murder in the news media and from the Undead to the authentic dead (fictional but credible corpses) in popular culture.

Death and the dead are centrepieces in popular entertainment formats, such as television, film, novels and comic books and even the fashion industry. As such, they consistently raise questions of appropriateness regarding visibility, and they highlight a continuing discomfort with factual representations. Exposure to death, particularly violent death within popular culture, according to the National Institute of Mental Health, was incredibly high back in the mid-1990s with evidence suggesting that the average American, by the age of 16, had witnessed 18,000 murders on television (Kearl, 1995). It is likely that this number has increased since then. This of course does not include all the other deaths portrayed in television and film that are consumed by the under 16s, including parental death in multiple Disney films (Cox, Garrett, & Graham, 2005). Death and dead bodies may be uncomfortable, distasteful or even dread-inducing and fear-inducing, but they are far from being supressed or invisible within popular culture. Instead, death is embraced, every day and as ultimately inevitable, which is in distinct contrast to the commonly and persistently asserted belief that it is a 'socially repressed taboo subject'[2].

The human body as a window or metaphor for society even when dead is saturated with meaning and functions as a method for viewing humanity (Posel & Gupta, 2009). In the previous chapter, the dead (as embodied by the Undead) have been considered as mobilisers of morbid sensibility in morbid space. In this chapter, the authentic dead are used to explore how death is represented in popular culture and how this aids viewers to confront death and, thus, challenges the public wisdom of contemporary society being in death denial. By first engaging with existing death denial debates, the argument will draw on popular culture representations of the authentic dead in order to consider how the consuming gaze of the viewer normalises the dead and enables them to experience death vicariously. By losing their status as extraordinary, repellent and unusual, the authentic dead largely disengage controversy and are able to form a palatable and normative bridge between viewers, death and the dead particularly through the lens of the fictional scientific expert.

CONFRONTING DEATH THROUGH DENIAL

There is a long-established belief that the industrialised West comprises death denial societies who refuse, or at best struggle, to confront death. The concept of death denial was first popularised by Gorer in 1955, who asserted that for Western society (particularly the United States), death was an unmentionable albeit natural process riddled with anxiety. The link between anxiety and death was taken further by Becker's assertions in 1973 in *The Denial of Death*, which presented society as universally repressing not just fear but also a terror of death. Views on death denial were a popular occurrence during the 1970s with Dumont and Foss (1972) considering that death is denied and accepted, at least within the United States, whilst Aries (1975) and Illich (1976) argued society to be death-denying due to the medicalisation of death and the crisis of individualism in the 20th century. However, what none of these scholars successfully achieved is a working definition of what exactly they mean by 'death denial', and none creates an understanding applicable to a sociological stance. As a result, public wisdom that the West is full of death denial societies is highly problematic for what does death denial actually mean? Does it refer to complete denial of death within a society whereby it is not discussed and is made as invisible to the populace as possible? Alternatively, is death denial actually referring to death as a taboo where it is a topic that is socially and cultural forbidden to be discussed? Or does death denial simply refer to a societal distaste and discomfort in openly confronting death, making people unwilling to talk about it or to face the realities of disposing of the dead? Or, on the other hand, is death denial referring to death as an issue that is deeply repressed in order to cope with deeply-rooted cultural fears about mortality?

Death denial is rooted in a variety of arguments including the increasing medicalisation of death, the rise of individualism as well as various death-denying social practices within the funeral industry (Kellehear, 1984). However, the most expansive argument in support of the existence of a death denial society is founded on Becker's (1973) social psychological case where the universality of the fear of death or rather 'terror' of death underpinned his assertions for the existence of death denial society. He agreed with Zilboorg (1943: 465–467) that fear of death is universally present for 'No one is free of the fear of death... [it is] always present in our mental functioning' and that an ever-present fear of death is that it needs to be properly repressed in order for people to keep living; as such

> We are intent on mastering death.... A man will say, of course, that he knows he will die someday, but

> he does not really care… this is purely intellectual
> verbal admission. The affect of fear is repressed.
> (p. 468–471).

Marcuse (1962) even asserted that not being repressed is impossible for 'The brute fact of death denies once and for all the reality of a non-repressive existence' (p. 211). People accept the 'cultural programming that turns his nose where he is supposed to look; he doesn't bite the world off in one piece as a giant would, but in small manageable pieces, as a beaver does' (Becker, 1973: 23). So, according to scholars who support the death denial thesis, death is denied and repressed in order for individuals to live without being overwhelmed by fear although it is grappled with in small amounts when individuals are directly (and personally) affected by death.

With its origins in psychology and psychoanalysis, death denial as a concept poses problems for people outside of these disciplinary approaches, particularly members of the public and sociological scholars. This is because death denial in its original form is limited by its focus on interaction and generalisations of the individual without social context. As Kellehear (1984) points out, death denial 'is used indiscriminately to refer to any avoidance of reality' (p. 713) leaving it open to a range of possible different interpretations. Death denial can, therefore, according to Kellehear (1984: 714), mean the avoidance of the end of ego (Freud, 1915; Becker, 1973); avoidance of the prospect of separation (Dumont & Foss, 1972; Brown 1959); avoidance of ambiguous social relations (Weisman, 1972); or fear of death which is actually fear of dying leading to avoidance of certain images of dying. Consequently, the concept of a death denial society due to its origins in psychiatric work makes it an unsuitable sociological concept as it is 'too broad and various for specific application, accurate description and general usage' (Kellehear, 1984: 714).

A further notable problem with the death denial argument is that it has faced remarkably little cited opposition. As Zimmermann and Rodin (2004) highlight, the opposing stance to the term 'death denial society' has received markedly less attention, particularly by clinical publications. The result being that much scholarship surrounding death denial does not question its relevance, accuracy or boundaries. Therefore, the perception of a death denial society being universal within the West is being replicated and propagated across scholarly disciplines and the world media as well as to media consumers who embrace this idea as public knowledge. Acceptance of death denial has become so powerfully established in Western societal beliefs that movements have begun as a direct response. For example, the hospice and palliative care movement developed (in part) to address a death denial society was seen to be offering poor care for the dying. There is also the rise of death enthusiasts who promote talking about death in a positive and open way, such as through the rise of death cafés[3], the death positive movement led by groups, such as The Order of the Good Death[4] and a range of charities and forums around the globe supporting the bereaved.

Challenging the death denial thesis has proved difficult because it has become normalised and formed deeply held social norms and convictions underpinning individual perceptions within Western society. Sociologist Lofland (1979) poured scorn on the idea that death is taboo, and Kellehear (1984) took up this rallying cry to analyse the public embrace of death denial (as already outlined). However, it was Walter (1991) who expanded the scrutiny of death denial to consider the question of death as taboo and confronted debates about death denial by challenging the interchangeable usage of death denial and death as taboo. Walter addressed the question of whether death is taboo and, if so, in what sense? And if death is not taboo, then why the frequent announcements that it is? He is unique in his approach to death denial by explicitly examining taboo, which is commonly bound up in the language of fear of death, and death avoidance arguments that define death society. Walter (1991) suggested that the death taboo is now crumbling and that death is hidden, not forbidden. He also argued that taboo is limited to influential groups, such as the media and the medical profession, and there is a loss of language for talking about death, so it is an uncomfortable topic in conversation. Finally, Walter points out that all societies accept and deny death, so death denial thesis scholars pick what fits their views and that it is the modern individual, not modern society, that denies death. Walter's (1991) claims about death taboo and death denial are crucial in regard to confronting death and examining the relationship between death, the dead and popular culture. Morbid sensibilities mobilised by a globally consumed popular culture reflect two key facets of Walter's argument, namely that death taboo is crumbling and that all societies both deny and accept death. In popular culture, representations of the dead challenge the notion that death is taboo or that death denial extends entirely across society by the intimate portrayals of death and corpses.

Confronting death through popular culture is valuable in engaging sociological thinking amongst people and challenging the public wisdom of death denial society. Durkin (2003) also reflects this in his short but significant chapter on death, dying and the dead in popular culture writing that the:

> thanatological elements of popular culture… help us to redefine death as something other than terror, and enjoyment of these themes requires some detachment on the part of the individual…[and] that we may be more accepting of death, dying and the dead because of our frequent exposure to these phenomena through our popular culture. (p.48)

For Durkin, popular culture portrayals of death and the dead have an important role to play in exposing individuals to death. Popular culture portrayals of death and the dead actively create a morbid space (Penfold-Mounce, 2015) in which to explore morbid sensibilities (see Chapter 4). Popular culture might not create a conversational language to talk about death (Walter, 1991), but it creates a *space*, namely a morbid space, in which death and the dead can allow the viewer to deny and accept the viewer and challenge any perceptions that death is taboo. Popular culture representations of death and dead is a vehicle for morbid sensibility and death enthusiasm. In the fictional, apparently frivolous realm of popular culture, individuals can choose to consume death and the dead for entertainment and explore the morbid and macabre. Portrayals of death and the dead in popular culture allow the line of reasoning that thanatological content can confront and 'socially neutralize death' and make it entertaining and enjoyable. This can even be understood to suggest that exposure to death and the dead in popular culture can have therapeutic effects (Khapaeva, 2017: 11–12), meaning that substantial viewing by individuals can diminish any 'primordial terror' as it is less frightening than real death (Durkin, 2003: 47). Death and the dead in popular culture therefore perform a critical function, as a mechanism in the disintegration and undermining of the death denial thesis and lingering belief in the death taboo.

GAZING UPON THE AUTHENTIC DEAD

Opportunities to gaze upon the dead are readily available in contemporary popular culture, particularly the authentic dead, who differ from the Undead as they are fictional but credible corpses. The authentic dead are numerous and displayed in varied degrees of graphic intimacy, but all are intended to draw the viewer's gaze. It is this gaze, which becomes a vehicle for agency of the authentic dead, who are able to influence and confront the individual with social and cultural issues whilst gazing upon mortality. The concept of the gaze has been used and interpreted in a variety of ways by different scholars, ranging from the feminist view on the male gaze developed in film studies and first published in 1975 (Mulvey, 1989), to the forensic gaze in crime drama (Pierson, 2010). In this chapter the gaze adopts and adapts Foucault's clinical gaze where the patient's body is 'read' and interpreted by a doctor creating a penetrating form of observation. Here the authentic dead are read by the gazer through a lens created by portrayals of the professional scientific gaze. To Foucault, power and knowledge can be attained through the gaze for there is no such thing as 'just a gaze', for it is able to be

> An inspecting gaze, a gaze which each individual
> under its weight will end by interiorizing to the
> point that he is his own overseer, each individual
> thus exercising this surveillance over, and against
> himself. A superb formula: power exercise
> continuously and for what turns out to be
> minimum cost. (Foucault, 1980: 155)

As such, the gaze upon the authentic dead provides the gazer with significant information and insights about the subject. To gaze upon death has been noted as acceptable in relation to artistic work by Bronfen (1992), who highlights that death in artwork is acceptable and this is echoed by the gaze upon popular culture portrayals of the dead. In both artwork and popular culture, the gaze is invited to look upon death and the dead in a realm that is defined by not being real life. The unreal morbid space of popular culture encourages consuming the dead for pleasure or entertainment is consolidated as death is experienced by proxy and, therefore, in a safe and acceptable way.

In the previous chapter, the Undead were used to propose and explore the concepts of safe and provocative morbid space for morbid sensibilities. The intention here is to build on these concepts through the authentic dead as a counterpart to their popular culture Undead cousins and to explore how they provide a gazeable morbid space that allows morbid sensibility to challenge perceptions of death taboo and death denial. The authentic dead differ from the Undead in that they are fake dead bodies, but they are convincingly lifelike. Sometimes they are life-sized models that can be dissected and convince the viewer that they are a human cadaver, but at other times they are live models or actors (known colloquially as corpse actors who do are doing corpse duty[5]) who literally 'play dead' in television and films and in the fashion industry. The authentic dead, in contrast to the Undead entertaining corpse, mostly appear in crime-focused television shows where they lie inanimate. They are a vital prop and critical lynchpin to the unfolding storyline and dominate crime drama, particularly police procedurals where a murder or unexpected death is central to the plot. An important characteristic of the authentic dead is that they will not suddenly become a vampire or zombie or rise from the dead. They are corpses within entertainment but are not the Undead. Two illustrations will be included here to explore the gaze and the authentic dead, firstly via the television show *Six Feet Under*, and secondly within the fashion industry using Foltyn's (2009) concept of corpse chic.

To gaze upon the authentic dead is to look upon the ordinary and expected (if you are watching a crime drama, murder victims are rife) and still be entertained. They encapsulate the atrocity exhibition of wound culture (Seltzer, 1998) that manifests itself in popular culture, from fashion to comic strips and from novels to video games, along with television and film, all of which embrace the authentic corpse. The authentic dead therefore emphasises a crossing point between pleasure and being disconcerted and disturbed. It encapsulates the morbid and the macabre and is 'more than a taste for senseless violence' (Seltzer, 1998: 21). In comparison to the Undead, the authentic dead do not reanimate although occasionally they do rise and talk but only as part of a surreal scene, a live character's imagination or a flashback (*Six Feet Under*, 2001–2005). Their role varies depending on the storyline in which they play a role. Sometimes, they are portrayed in a humorous slapstick manner such as in *Weekend at Bernie's* (1989; 1993), where Bernie the 'authentic dead' still fools many characters into believing he is still alive. In comedy drama like *Swiss Army Man* (2016), the lead protagonist Hank develops a friendship with a dead body and discovers he can manipulate the corpse like a Swiss army knife.

Using the dead as entertainment within popular culture particularly in television and film is commonplace. However, some instances of engaging with death are more notable than others in inviting the gaze to linger upon the dead. A landmark popular culture engagement with the dead that gathered many accolades is the HBO television series *Six Feet Under*, which ran for five seasons from 2001–2005. The show overtly tackles mortality through portrayals of the life and relationships of the Fisher family who run a Los Angeles funeral home. Largely, the show is a conventional family drama, tackling issues such as interpersonal relationships, infidelity and religion; however, it is unique in its unremitting focus on death. From this position, *Six Feet Under* was able to explore death and the dead from assortment of angles including personal, religious and philosophical. Each episode opens with a death, which ranges from a heart attack to murder and from a sudden infant death syndrome (SIDS) to death in an industrial dough-making machine. The death usually sets the tone for each episode, allowing the characters to reflect on their current fortunes and misfortunes in a way that is illuminated by the death and its aftermath. For example, in Episode 8, Season 4, James Dubois Marshall dies in the opening scene; he gets up goes through his daily motions, drives to the Fishers' home, arranges a goodbye note on his car dashboard and dies. His death is mirrored in the Fisher family's need to regain control over aspects of their lives. They are all stuck in patterns of doubt, dissatisfaction, fear, submission and are desperate to break free. For Ruth, the Fisher family matriarch, she relives the loneliness of her first marriage in her second one, while for Claire, the daughter, it is to achieve orgasm where she needs to lose control. Meanwhile, Nate and Brenda, the son and his partner, need to slacken their grip on their life situation from which they cannot currently move on and for David, the other Fisher son, it is to stop fooling his family and friends that he is ok as his sister Claire describes: 'If you were any more controlled, you'd be a sculpture'.

Through its unflinching focus on human mortality and the lives of those who deal with death and the dead on a daily basis, *Six Feet Under* is a catalyst for morbid sensibility as a vehicle within popular culture and defined morbid space to consider social issues of kinship, sex and sexuality, age and loneliness, to name but a few. Much like how the Undead in their fantasy-horror setting provide safe and provocative morbid spaces in order to explore morbid sensibilities (see Chapter 5), *Six Feet Under* does the same but achieves this through the gaze upon the authentic dead. In seeking to entertain the viewer, *Six Feet Under* also shocks and provokes using a recurring plot device whereby a central character converses with the person who died at the beginning of the episode, while they are being embalmed or planning or during the funeral. This surreal engagement with the authentic dead explores key issues such are relationships or cultural fears defines *Six Feet Under* as a hugely unusual and fearless cultural engagement with death and corpses at the turn of the 21st century. As show creator, Alan Ball, reflects in relation to the concept of the show:

> Who are these people who are funeral directors that we hire to face death for us? What does that do to their own lives—to grow up in a home where there are dead bodies in the basement, to be a child and walk in on your father with a body lying on a table opened up and him working on it? What does that do to you?[6]

The Fisher family are consistently represented to experience various crises, many of which are relatable to viewers' lives, but they are experienced in direct relation to their death industry environment and the grief they have experienced. They, along with the authentic dead, are used to mobilise the viewer's morbid sensibility and to explore wider cultural and societal issues in relation to and through death and loss.

Six Feet Under achieved more than just high viewing figures and an avid fanbase. According to Alan Ball, it sought to fulfil a purpose of exploring how individuals experience death and the dead through the death industry. The very title of the show, *Six Feet Under*, refers to

> not only to being buried as a dead body is buried, but to primal emotions and feelings running under the surface. When one is surrounded by death—to counterbalance that, there needs to be a certain intensity of experience, of needing to escape. It's Nate with his womanizing—it's Claire and her sexual experimentation—it's Brenda's sexual compulsiveness—it's David having sex with a male

hooker in public—it's Ruth having several affairs—
it's the life force trying to push up through all of
that suffering and grief and depression.[7]

Six Feet Under is an explicit popular culture challenge to
the idea of death denial and death as taboo. It used death and
the authentic dead to directly engage with mortality and led to
other shows pushing boundaries of death representation. For
example, *Pushing Daisies* (2007–2009), which blurred genres
by creating a forensic fairy tale playing with the boundaries
of authentic corpses whereby life and death could be granted
and taken away at the touch of Ned, the piemaker. Although
this show was shorter-lived than *Six Feet Under* and did not
achieve the same depth of engagement with morbid sensibilities, it was a safe morbid space in which to examine death
and the dead.

Gazing upon the authentic dead is not limited to television and film but extends into still images that blur death
and beauty within the fashion industry. Foltyn (2009) conceptualises the use of the authentic dead in fashion as 'corpse
chic', drawing attention to how the representation of the dead
are predominantly female and are heavily objectified. The
authentic dead as corpse chic has moved from the margins
to the centre of fashion drawing with it the consumer's gaze.
Fashion pictures use corpse chic to entice the consumer to
spend by capturing the gaze through representations of the
authentic dead, sometimes situated alongside celebrities (i.e.,
the Marc Jacobs fashion shoot in 2014 where singer Miley
Cyrus posed alongside authentic dead models) and have
apparently all met violent ends. For example, the 2006 Jimmy Choo advertisement where an apparently dead woman is
half in and half out of a car boot in the desert with a man,
spade in hand, sits next to her and the Duncan Quinn suit
advertisement in 2008 where a stylish man appears to have

strangled an underwear-clad woman draped over a car bonnet. Not only are the authentic dead in fashion predominantly women, they are also victims of male violence and fetishized. *W Magazine* illustrated this in 2007 and released a fashion story featuring the model Doutzen Kroes, who was posed in a woodland setting semi-naked and apparently dead in a fetishized manner with teddy bears. This image was striking for its links to a sexual subculture known as 'furries' where people wear fur costumes to have sex (Foltyn, 2009: 382). Kroes was styled to represent the ultimate vulnerable, female dead body. She became the epitome of the stylised authentic dead and reflects that corpse chic offers 'some arresting if unsettling portrayals of the dead body that drive consumers to spend' whilst imbuing the gaze with 'seductively disturbing images' (Foltyn, 2009: 380).

Responses to the use of the authentic dead in fashion has been mixed, ranging from being considered tasteless to daring, risky and boundary-breaking and therefore highly controversial. The New Zealand boutique *Superette*, in 2009, was considered distasteful as it glamourized the female authentic dead through various violent deaths, such as impalement on fence railings to being crushed by an elevator, under the tagline: 'Be caught dead in it'. In contrast, *Vice* magazine's 2013 photoshoot that replicated famous female writers' suicides as a 'Last words' was reviled to the extent that *Vice* apologised and removed the images from the website. Interestingly, no apologies were requested from Turkish designer Başak Cankeş at The Bashaques show at the Istanbul Fashion Week in 2017 although her catwalk show invited the audience to gaze upon an apparent massacre with models covered in fake blood stepping over prone corpses with one woman dressed in a nude suit wielding a bloody sword[8]. In contrast, the authentic dead as part of corpse chic did come under fire when *America's Next Top Model* television series in 2007 featured an episode where contestants had to pose as murder victims. Comments from the judges included that one contestant who had been stabbed did not look dead enough whilst another was told 'death becomes you, young lady' and still another was told: 'the look on your face is just extraordinary. Very beautiful and dead.'[9] The episode received criticism although no apology was issued due to its connotations of violence against women being beautiful, including from Sonia Ossorio, President of the New York City chapter of the National Organization for Women. Ossorio expressed concern that fashion shoot was 'supremely ironic, when it's a show geared toward women about women, and about glamour.'[10] The authentic dead in fashion are interwoven with controversy and criticism and allow for morbid sensibility to explore the boundaries between beauty, death and violence.

The majority of the authentic dead in fashion are women, but there are some instances where men are used, such as the image of dancer/model Kevin Federline with a slashed throat taken by celebrity photographer Steven Klein. This portrait photograph focused on the tipped back head exposing the slashed throat of Federline was taken specifically for the 'Face of Fashion' exhibit at the National Portrait Gallery in 2007. This photograph is intriguing as it captures a popular culture celebrity figure, which crosses into artwork. The Federline image allows speculation that the male celebrity authentic dead is deemed worthy of becoming art and drawing the gaze of the educated and artistic. Meanwhile, the female authentic dead is left vulnerable to the voyeuristic gaze that is fetishized and objectified within the realm of popular culture in order to sell a product to consumers. Ultimately, whether the authentic dead are male or female in television shows, movies or in fashion shoots, they offer an alternative to the public wisdom that death denial is widespread and that death is taboo for they attract the gaze from across the globe and are visually consumed.

CRIME, FORENSICS AND THE AUTHENTIC DEAD: THE EXPERT LENS

Although the authentic dead appear in popular culture forms such as fashion shoots, films and video games, they are nowhere more visible, naturalised and acceptable or as central and essential to storytelling than in the global plethora of crime drama and forensic science television shows. The authentic dead, in this context, are truly 'pop culture's new star' (Foltyn, 2008b: 154) where they link widespread fascination with death and the dead and lead the gaze into the forensic science setting (McIlwain, 2005). In crime dramas, forensic science is an essential component to the plot, which also defines how the authentic dead are gazed upon. In movies and television shows, forensics engage with death and the dead through the expert professional lens of science. The crime drama genre does not expect its viewers to disassociate themselves from authentic life like horror/fantasy do with the Undead. Instead, crime drama wants the viewer to believe they are seeing what really happens behind closed doors, that they are witnessing the gritty reality of investigating and solving crime in contemporary society. The use of forensics has, therefore, become a critical facet of the plot involving victims (who are predominantly, although not exclusively, the authentic dead) and also characters who include, but are not limited to, pathologists and coroners, blood splatter and ballistics experts and even forensic anthropologists. All such characters specialise in understanding the dead in a professional scientific or pseudo-scientific manner particularly in relation to crime. They provide depth to the storyline and form normalising scientific barriers, softening the realities of death for the viewer. Forensics and forensic scientists enable the viewer to gaze upon the dead through the professional eyes of science but most importantly, they enable the dead to have agency. The authentic dead speak from beyond the grave communicating to the experts and, therefore, the viewers, what happened to them and how they died.

Images of forensic science have become integral to our visual culture (Foltyn, 2008c) particularly popular culture and are conveyed through the representation of a variety of experts all of whom consistently iterate the capabilities of forensics to solve crime and bring perpetrators to justice (Doherty, 2003, B15–16). The most common expert is the police forensic examiner or crime scene investigator such as portrayed in television shows, such as *CSI: Crime Scene Investigation* (2000–2015), *NCIS* (2003–present), *Cold Case* (2003–2010), *Waking the Dead* (2000-), *The Body Farm* (2011) and *Silent Witness* (1996-). Perhaps nowhere is normalisation of death more evident than in the *CSI: Crime Scene Investigation* television series, which became a franchise. The original CSI show based in Las Vegas spawned various successful spin-off series: *CSI: Miami* (2002–2012), *CSI: New York* (2004–2013) and *CSI: Cyber* (2015–2016), which together achieved an impressive longevity of 16 years. This period was defined by repeated portrayals of an exaggerated dramatic vision of forensic science and the authentic dead. The cadaver became not only an engaging and acceptable forensic tool (Timmermans, 2006), whose appearance was anticipated and expected by viewers, but also a key character. The authentic dead in the CSI shows were more than just a passive prop; they were active in their engagement with the gaze of the viewer and the storyline itself. The authentic dead attained not only a central recurring role in CSI episode plots but became accessible, acceptable corpses that entertained whilst stimulating morbid sensibility of viewers.

The portrayals of the authentic dead and the forensic techniques, experts and processes that surround them in order to understand death has led to the so-called 'CSI effect'[11]. This effect refers to the impact of forensic science representation in popular culture upon public perceptions and understandings of criminal justice as well as introducing forensic science terminology and concepts into popular discourse. Importantly, popular perceptions of forensic science capabilities in solving crime, especially murders as represented in popular culture, are in direct conflict with reality. For example, estimates suggest that 40 percent of the science on CSI does not exist and much of the rest is performed in a manner that crime lab personnel can only dream about[12]. Further misrepresentations of forensic science in popular culture reinforce in the public mind that physical evidence is reliable and always present, unlike absent or flawed human witnesses (Thornton, 2002). Forensic science in popular culture is shown to be not only science but also a super science that can aid in the conviction of murderers and violent criminals even after their death or the demise of the victim. As a result, the authentic dead are active promoters of the idea that science and the police are virtually infallible (Deutsch & Cavender, 2008). They also play a role in conveying that forensic science is glamourous and sexy, making working with the dead outside of popular culture portrayals a desirable environment, as reflected by the rise in demand for forensic courses in Higher Education Institutions (Penfold-Mounce, 2015).

Forensic science-driven popular culture and its focus on the authentic dead combined with the CSI effect creates a morbid space that is specifically viewed through an 'expert lens'. The expert lens allows for the viewer's gaze to be softened and protected by viewing the dead and death through the eyes of the expert or professional forensic scientist. By seeing the dead through the eyes of the expert, the viewer sees through the lens of science. The acceptance of viewing the dead in an often graphic fashion within a forensic science setting turns the corpse into a matter of routine and its openness achieves unremarkable normative status. Many crime dramas, of which *CSI* is a quintessential example, construct an expert lens that blends scenes with graphic visual portrayals of autopsies and fictional forensics equipment. For example, in *CSI: Miami*, a virtual autopsy is conducted by combining scans in order to work around the widow of the victim using a court injunction to prevent a physical autopsy ('Deep Freeze', Season 6, Episode 5). The expert lens empowers the viewer by allowing them to access perceived truth through forensics and the authentic display agency back in stimulating morbid sensibility in the viewer. The expert scientist lens not only provides intimacy, as the viewer can right inside the corpse in graphic detail, but also protects by maintaining distance from the realities of death. For example, in popular culture, in forensic scenes, there is no smell of decomposition; no splatter of body fluids or sound of gas release or crack of bones being broken to access organs. The viewer's gaze does not have to experience the physicality of conducting an autopsy for which morticians and pathologists have to have tangible strength. Instead, the expert lens allows the viewer to confront and gaze upon a more sanitised, albeit convincingly graphic and gruesome, vision of the dead.

The authentic dead through the expert lens offers individuals an imagined sense of control over not only crime and criminality (as crime scene investigators and police always get their man) but also over death itself. The authentic dead in television shows using forensics experts provide

> visual access but separate the viewer from the
> reality of death. Consumption is through the
> eyes and the sounds are edited and occasionally
> interspersed with music montages to make the
> corpse both separate and more palatable to the
> viewer. (Penfold-Mounce, 2015: 27)

Confronting the dead through the visualisation of the authentic dead is aided by representations of forensic scientists who consistently articulate their thoughts and findings aloud about the victim. This is effective in crime drama as it allows the crime experts to outline key plot devices relating to the authentic dead whilst using layman accessible scientific language and jargon. The expert lens allows the viewer's gaze, intertwined with the language of investigation (Foucault, 1973; Pierson, 2010), to deliberate death through the mediumship of the authentic dead and protected from the realities of corpses and decomposition. The expert lens allows the authentic dead to exert their agency as part of entertainment rather than an object of revulsion and fear or an educational tool. As such, it provides distance for the viewer from true intimacy with the dead but graphic insight and access is granted through the expert lens of science.

The expert lens provides specific protection in popular culture-defined morbid space, but this does not extend to news media coverage of the dead. The dead in news media differ to those in popular culture as they are the actual dead and not the authentic dead. Furthermore, although they are often associated with words and comments from experts and the journalists writing the story are professionals, images of the dead remain shocking; they are too revealing and an uncomfortable reminder of mortality. The dead in the media outside of popular culture do not challenge death denial or death taboo in the way that the authentic dead can or how the Undead provide safe and provocative morbid space for morbid sensibilities. Instead, the news mediated dead remain controversial and uncomfortable viewing. Arguably, they actually reinforce the death denial thesis by reminding consumers of their mortality and the horrors of death without the softening barrier supplied by the fun and frivolous characteristics of popular culture. The actual corpse requires distance and respect with a distinct lack of intimacy for the viewer. Furthermore, without the expert lens of science as provided in popular culture, the gaze upon the news-mediated dead lacks a degree of respectability and reinforces fear and discomfort about mortality, supporting the death denial thesis. The actual dead do not entertain like the authentic dead but shock and horrify. They provide good reason to the viewer to repress and deny death and adopt the belief that death is, and should be, taboo.

CONCLUSION

In our visually dominated contemporary society, the ability to confront death and gaze upon the dead within popular culture or in the news is simple and often unavoidable. The authentic dead within popular culture make death and corpses commonplace, easily consumed and ultimately entertainment. The authentic dead are well-established as ordinary and mundane in popular culture appearing as props or characters designed to be graphic, shocking and sometimes distasteful. Consequently, debates surrounding whether Western society is in death denial or that death is taboo are challenged by popular culture representations of the authentic dead. The authentic dead build a societally palatable and normative bridge (although this does not mean it lacks controversy as evident in the fashion industry) that allows morbid sensibilities to be mobilised without fear of censure or breaking perceived social norms regarding death denial and taboo. In attempting realism, the authentic dead create a morbid space in which death denial is contested and the visibility of the dead through the gaze stimulates morbid sensibilities such as death, violence and women. A crucial factor in gazing upon the authentic dead is the plethora of portrayals they have in crime drama representations where the expert lens provides protection for the viewer. Morbid sensibilities are filtered through the expert lens allowing the viewer to confront the dead and stare death in the face within the safe confines of popular culture defined morbid space where considering death has no direct consequences.

NOTES

1. Troyer, J. (2014, 10 April) Death isn't taboo, we're just not encouraged to talk about it. https://theconversation.com/death-isnt-taboo-were-just-not-encouraged-to-talk-about-it-25001 [accessed 12/9/2017]

2. Troyer, J. (2014, 10 April). Death isn't taboo, we're just not encouraged to talk about it. https://theconversation.com/death-isnt-taboo-were-just-not-encouraged-to-talk-about-it-25001[accessed 12/9/2017]

3. The first death café was held in London in Sept 2011. By 2017, more than 4,000 have been held since all over the UK http://deathcafe.com/

4. Founded in January 2011 by Caitlin Doughty, a mortician. http://www.orderofthegooddeath.com/death-positive

5. Chozick, A. (2011, 9 February) Working Stiffs: Playing Dead on TV can keep a career on life support. https://www.wsj.com/articles/SB10001424052748703439504576116092672612366 [accessed 21/09/2017]

6. Ball, Alan. Six Feet Under: The Complete Series – "In Memoriam" featurette (DVD). HBO Home Video.

7. Ball, Alan (writer/director). Six Feet Under: The Complete Fifth Season – "Everyone's Waiting" audio commentary (DVD). HBO Home Video.

8. Anon. (2011, 15 September). Turkish designer's runway show resembles a massacre as models covered in fake blood step over 'bodies' on the catwalk at Istanbul Fashion Week. http://www.dailymail.co.uk/femail/article-4885582/Istanbul-Fashion-Week-resembles-bloody-massacre.html [accessed 21/09/2017]

9. Cochran, K. (2007, 27 March) Model of Bad Taste. https://www.theguardian.com/media/2007/mar/27/broadcasting.comment [accessed 19/7/2017]

10. Snarker, D. (2007, 27 March) Death does not become her: America's Next Top Model crosses the line. http://www.afterellen.com/general-news/7634-death-does-not-become-her-americas-next-top-model-crosses-the-line [accessed 19/7/2017].

11. Anon. (2007, 23 March) Tyra's rapped on gory TV pix. *The NY Daily* http://www.nydailynews.com/entertainment/tv-movies/tyra-rapped-gory-tv-pix-article-1.217954 [accessed 19/7/2017].

12. Lafsky, M. (2007, 26 March) America's Next Top Controversy: ANTM Features 'Murdered' Models. *The Huffington Post* http://www.huffingtonpost.com/eat-the-press/2007/03/26/americas-next-top-contro_e_44291.html [accessed 19/7/2017]

13. The origins of the term 'CSI effect' are murky although there is agreement that it started to be used following the global popularity of *CSI: Crime Scene Investigation* in the early 2000s.

14. Cole, S. and Dioso, R. (2005, 13 May). Law and the Lab: Do TV Shows Really Affect How Juries Vote? Let's Look at the Evidence. *Wall Street Journal*. Retrieved from http://truthinjustice.org/law-lab.htm p.13.

6

REFLECTIONS ON ENCOUNTERING DEATH AND THE DEAD IN POPULAR CULTURE

In Shakespeare's "Hamlet", death is referred to with dread and fear as the 'undiscovered country from whose bourn, no traveller returns.' (Act 3, Scene 1). Written sometime between 1599 and 1602, the play portrays death as fully able to excite anxiety and trepidation, bordering at times on terror. Shakespeare's work remains impressively modern despite its age and, although it might now be considered high culture, up until the 19th century, his work was very much part of popular theatre (Storey, 2015). So, arguably, Shakespeare's Hamlet is an early (non-mediated) form of popularist culture that tackled death and mortality, which resonates with contemporary popular culture representations of the same issues some five centuries later. Consumable culture on a mass popularist scale vary across time, but themes with which they engage are impressively constant. Prince Hamlet of Denmark actively embraces the big social questions held around mortality. He does this despite his fears and does not deny or repress death, reflecting a willingness to deliberate and face up to death, the dead and human mortality. In fact, he quite literally encounters the dead in the form of Yorick's skull and his father's ghost. Although this book chooses not to focus on the paranormal as a dimension in which to meet the dead, the dead themselves can be encountered in many forms within contemporary popular culture. Death remains, as Hamlet describes, an 'undiscovered country' and yet every human ultimately enters it. In the 21st century, as we are beckoned towards it, death and the dead in popular culture provides a crucial morbid space in which to mobilise our morbid sensibilities rooted in lingering cultural and societally held fears about mortality.

In the opening chapter of this book, the concept of agency was offered as the argument that binds together death, the dead and popular culture. It aimed to suggest that the entertaining and sometimes fictional dead are influential and actively engaging with the living from beyond the grave. Death and the dead in contemporary times cannot be effectively avoided as popular culture provides a far-reaching and accessible morbid space in which mortality can be explored without impunity or derision. The following four chapters sought to illustrate the agency of the dead through posthumous celebrity careers, myths of organ transplantation, the Undead and the authentic dead. In this final chapter, the underlying theme of the agency of the dead is used to reflect upon how popular culture as highly accessible entertainment makes encountering death and the dead into a prime site for considering questions and igniting debates surrounding cultural and individual beliefs about mortality. Finally, thoughts regarding the distinctive contribution that has been made by this book to scholarship, particularly in the field of sociology and death studies, are reflected upon in regard to choosing to study death and the dead within the context of popular culture.

ACCESSIBLE DEATH

Popular culture provides an accessible space within which to encounter the dead. As Woodthorpe (2010: 283) wrote, 'Death in the twenty-first century is immensely accessible. In books, on television, in film, on the internet, in newspapers and magazines, it is plentifully available in popular culture'. Portrayals of death and dead bodies in popular culture range from being graphic and gruesome to playful and creative, but at all times, they are flexible enough to allow the formation of a space that is specifically morbid in nature. Popular culture does not shy away from the morbid and macabre but embraces and revels in it. The portrayal of death and the dead celebrates them and offers the chance for wide consumption through an array of creative forms that engage with the gaze of the viewer. Death ranges from being portrayed for children as a person (see *Horrible Histories* television series' recurring sketch Stupid Deaths, 2009–2013), to being a critical narrative feature where a key character dies (see the death of Professor Albus Dumbledore in the novel, *Harry Potter and the Half-Blood Prince*, 2005). In another example, death and the dead underpin the purpose of the story itself (see the novel *A Monster Calls*, 2011), or a dead body is the lynchpin and catalyst for the purpose of the story narrative (see any crime drama or literature containing a murder). Easily accessible encounters with death and the dead body in popular culture are consistent in their availability and being strikingly explicit and in intimate detail. Any individual consumer can encounter the dead and stare death in the face enabling their gaze to allow vicarious experiences of mortality.

Popular culture enables its consumers to easily encounter death and the dead face-to-face without the ethical dilemmas surrounding granting access to actual corpses. Instead, it presents the viewer with representations of death and the dead in a cultural form that is defined by being fun, entertaining and larger than life. Popular culture is a hub through which death and the dead collide with the living; it is a dynamic realm from which the dead can engage with the living forming an imaginative space where themes surrounding mortality can be raised and examined by scholars or lay people alike. The diverse number of forms in which death is portrayed and how the dead are represented in popular culture is worthy of consideration as part of the emerging cult of death (Khapaeva, 2017). What becomes clear from popular culture representations of death and the dead is that it is a more ordinary, banal and normative topic than is commonly perceived by public wisdom. The long-standing public wisdom that Western culture is comprised of death denial societies where death is taboo is contestable by the sheer volume and global presence of representations of death and the dead, albeit in fictional form. Consuming the dead through culture that is populist suggests that death is far from being rare or uncomfortable territory. Death is commonplace and everywhere within popular consumable cultural forms, making encounters with the dead both normal and banal.

The range of ways in which it is possible to encounter death and the dead within popular culture illuminates a significant route to making death accessible to a mass audience. Watching people die and be autopsied, reanimating as the Undead, seeing dead celebrities continuing their careers or watching body parts from the dead find new lives via transplantation all make death and the dead easily accessible. Death is not hidden or denied but is instead showcased to the consuming gaze of the viewer. Popular culture is a springboard into the realm of mortality and the questions, hopes and fears that viewers hold regarding themselves and their loved ones. Death and the dead in popular culture reinforce the argument that they possess agency and that this agency grants depth and significance to a cultural form that is often perceived as simply frivolous and superficial entertainment. The innate power of popular culture is that it neutralises discomfort with death. It is a safe, fictional, unreal space; it is a lens through which to witness human mortality. As such, it is a space where a globally-consumed phenomenon allows morbid inclinations to be explored within a framework of morbid space.

THOUGHTS ON USING POPULAR CULTURE IN DEATH SCHOLARSHIP

In choosing to address death and corpses through popular culture, this book has sought to suggest not only the ability of the dead to exert power and influence on living consumers but also the value of using popular source materials. Researching popular culture falls within the remit of what is perceived as a 'glossy topic', which refers to issues that are of public *interest* but are not considered to be of public *value* (Beer & Penfold-Mounce, 2010: 363; Penfold-Mounce, 2015). These topics, predominant in popular culture, attract a large proportion of people's interest, but it does not follow that that value will be placed upon academic work studying it. In fact, the opposite can sometimes be the case with political leaders, policy-makers and university governing bodies reaching the same conclusions (Beer & Penfold-Mounce, 2010). In studying popular culture alongside death and the dead, it might appear that the superficial and frivolous is being used to engage with a weighty and worthy topic. However, this book seeks to suggest that although popular culture may appear superficial, frivolous, fun and entertaining, it has something significant to say about society. Just as myths remain important in the age of science as a network of symbols for interpreting the world (Midgley, 2004), popular culture is a crucial site for cross-cultural and cross-generational understandings of global society. Or, as Lipsitz (1990: 20) noted, what may seem like 'a sideshow can sometimes be the main event'. Although he was writing about music, the same case can be made for publications that 'anoint the famous and analyse their meaning' (Kitch & Hume, 2008: 93). Looking at dead celebrity careers, myths about organ transplantation, the Undead, and the authentic dead does possess an element of entertainment and even amusement. However, this should not detract from these popular culture illustrations as a valuable source of data for the sociological imagination in relation to death and the dead. For many people, popular culture embodies central tales for understanding society and the world around them. Just because popular culture is accessible and encourages encounters with the dead, leading to vast worldwide consumption, does not lessen its value.

As a consequence of the considerable power of popular culture in exposing individuals to multiple forms of death and the dead, this book has highlighted the need for more interdisciplinary research into death and the dead on a populist cultural level. Drawing on popular culture contributes to balancing out the plethora of highly insightful and policy-based research into death, dying and grieving. It also emphasises that more conceptual, theoretical and empirical work linking death and the dead to 'glossy topics' (Penfold-Mounce, 2015) is needed. It also reiterates the argument of the value to be found in academic research into the popular and the 'glossy' (Beer & Penfold-Mounce, 2010; Penfold-Mounce, 2015) to death scholarship. It would seem that frivolous sources of culture have vital data for social science researchers to engage with core issues within contemporary society. Consequently, it is essential that the frivolous and the glossy is taken seriously as valuable data in order to avoid failing to consider a key creator, catalyst and propagator of wider societal and cultural issues (see Penfold-Mounce, 2015). In order drive this agenda forward the aim of this book has been twofold:

1. to fill the gap in existing death scholarship by considering representations of death and the dead in popular culture beyond existing studies

2. to argue that the dead have agency within popular culture

These aims have been achieved, firstly, through illustrations of the economic and symbolic value and power of the dead via posthumous celebrity careers (Chapter 2) and organ transplantation mythology (Chapter 3). Secondly, these aims have been achieved via a conceptual framework of popular culture as a 'safe' and 'provocative' morbid space in which morbid sensibility is mobilised (Chapter 4) and via how these concepts offer a challenge to the death denial thesis and death taboo (Chapter 5). In all these different popular culture forms, the portrayals of death and the dead enable individual and culturally held fears about death to be considered in an entertaining manner with the assurance that it is ultimately only fiction, a representation of death and mortality. Notably, Chapters 4 and 5, which offer an expansion of the concept of morbid space to include 'safe' and 'provocative' space and the introduction of morbid sensibility, are of particular significance because they provide a versatile framework applicable to a wide variety of other 'glossy' topics (Beer & Penfold-Mounce, 2010) and their engagement with death.

CONCLUSION

Therefore, in conclusion, death in popular culture is not *the* end or even an end but a setting for the telling of vibrant stories, which inject agency into the dead. Popular culture allows for powerful visions of the dead to wield agency whereby they can influence the living. The massive consumption of so-called frivolous entertainment across the globe provides a lush environment that is ripe with potential within which to gaze upon and consume the demise of self and that of others. It is the ideal place in which to deliberate mortality and to examine perceptions of death and the dead. Through popular culture, Hamlet's 'undiscovered country' has never been more accessible in terms of the sheer range of portrayals and representations of possibilities surrounding death and the dead. Popular culture has not provided a bridge over the chasm between life and death into the 'undiscovered country', nor has it provided a passport and first-class return ticket allowing the individual to travel safely there and back again. Instead, popular culture has provided an immense window into death with safety glass fitted into an airtight frame. It allows people to see through it and examine in intimate detail the 'undiscovered country' of death where the dead dwell but are not contained.

REFERENCES

Akass, K., &McCabe, J. (Eds.), (2005). *Reading 'Six Feet Under': TV to die for*. London: IB Tauris.

Ambagtsheer, F., & Weimar, W. (2012). A criminological perspective: Why prohibition of organ trade is not effective and how the Declaration of Istanbul can move forward. *American Journal of Transplantation*, *12*(3), 571–575.

Auchter, J. (2017). On viewing: The politics of looking at the corpse. *Global Discourse*, *7*(2–3), 223–238.

Austin, E. (2015). Zombie culture: dissent, celebration and the carnivalesque in social spaces. In L. Hubner, M. Leaning & P. Manning (Eds.), *The zombie renaissance in popular culture* (pp. 174–190). UK: Palgrave Macmillan.

Bainbridge, D. (2002). *Intellectual property*. (5th ed.). London: Longman.

Barron, L. (2014). *Celebrity cultures: An introduction*. London: Sage.

Baudrillard, J. (1993). *Symbolic exchange and death*. London: Sage.

Beck, B. (2011). Fearless vampire kissers: Bloodsuckers we love in Twilight, True Blood and others. *Multicultural Perspectives*, *13*(2), 90–92.

Becker, E. (1973). *The denial of death*. New York, NY: Collier-Macmillan.

Becker, H. (1963). *Outsiders*. Glencoe, IL: Free Press of Glencoe.

Beer, D., & Burrows, R. (2010). The sociological imagination as popular culture. In J. Burnett, S. Jeffers & G. Thomas (Eds.), *New Social Connections* (pp. 233–252). London: Palgrave Macmillan.

Beer, D., & Penfold-Mounce, R. (2010). Researching glossy topics: the case of the academic study of celebrity. *Celebrity Studies*, *1*(3), 360–365.

Behuniak, S. M. (2011). The living dead? The construction of people with Alzheimer's disease as zombies. *Ageing and Society*, *31*(1), 70–92.

Bilewicz, M., Imhoff, R., & Drogosz, M. (2011). The humanity of what we eat: Conceptions of human uniqueness among vegetarians and omnivores. *European Journal of Social Psychology*, *41*, 201–209.

Boon, K. (2011). The zombie as other: Mortality and the monstrous in the post-nuclear age. In D. Christie & J. Lauro (Eds.), *Better off dead: The evolution of the zombie as post-human* (pp. 50–60). New York, NY: Fordham University.

Bronfen, E. (1992). *Over her dead body: Death, femininity and the aesthetic*. Manchester: Manchester University Press.

Brown, N. O. (1959). *Life against death: The psychoanalytical meaning of history*. Middletown, CT: Wesleyan University Press.

Brunt, S. (2015). Performing beyond the grave: The posthumous duet. In C. Strong & B. Lebrun (Eds.), *Death and the rock star* (pp. 165–176). Abingdon-on-Thames: Routledge.

Budiani-Saberi, D. A., & Delmonico, F. L. (2008). Organ trafficking and transplant tourism: a commentary on the global realities. *American Journal of Transplantation*, *8*(5), 925–929.

Cameron, J. S., & Hoffenberg, R. (1999). The ethics of organ transplantation reconsidered: Paid organ donation and the use of executed prisoners as donors. *Kidney international*, *55*(2), 724–732.

Campbell, P. O. (2013). Intersectionality bites: Metaphors of race and sexuality in HBO's True Blood. In M. Levina & D. M. T. Bui (Eds.), *Monster culture in the 21st century: A reader* (pp. 99–114). New York, NY: Bloomsbury Publishing.

Campion-Vincent, V. (2002). Organ theft narratives as medical and social critique. *Journal of Folklore Research*, *39*(1), 33–50.

Cashmore, E. (2014). *Celebrity culture*. (2nd ed.). Abingdon-on-Thames: Routledge.

Ciekawy, D., & Geschiere, P. (1998). Containing witchcraft: Conflicting scenarios in postcolonial Africa. *Africa Studies Review*, *41*(3), 1–14.

Cohen, J. J. (1996). *Monster theory: Reading culture*. Minneapolis, MN: University of Minnesota Press.

Comaroff, J. (1982). Medicine: symbol and ideology. In P. Wright & A. Treacher (Eds.), *The problem of medical knowledge* (pp. 49–68). Edinburgh: Edinburgh University Press.

Conrich, I. (2014). An infected population: Zombie culture and the modern monstrous. In L. Hubner, M. Leaning &

P. Manning (Eds.), *The zombie renaissance in popular culture* (pp. 15–25). Basingstoke: Palgrave Macmillan.

Cox, M., Garrett, E., & Graham, J. A. (2005). Death in Disney films: Implications for children's understanding of death. *Omega Journal of Death and Dying*, *50*(4), 267–280.

Davis, W. (2000). *Passage of darkness: The ethnobiology of the Haitian zombie*. Chapel Hill, NC: University of North Carolina Press.

Delmonico, F. L., Arnold, R., Scheper-Hughes, N., Siminoff, L. A., Kahn, J., & Youngner, S. J. (2002). Ethical incentives—not payment—for organ donation. *New England Journal of Medicine*, *346*(25), 2002–2005.

Deutsch, S. K., & Cavender, G. (2008). CSI and forensic realism. *Journal of Criminal Justice and Popular Culture*, *15*(1), 34–53.

Doherty, T. (2003). Cultural studies and 'Forensic Noir'. *Chronicle of Higher Education*, *50*(9), B15–16.

Donovan, P. (2002). Crime legends in a new medium: Fact, fiction and loss of authority. *Theoretical Criminology*, *6*(2), 189–215.

D'Rozario, D., & Bryant, F. (2013). The use of dead celebrity images in advertising and marketing—review, ethical recommendations and cautions for practitioners. *International Journal of Marketing Studies*, *5*(2), 1–10.

D'Rozario, D. (2016). Dead celebrity (Deleb) use in marketing: An initial theoretical exposition. *Psychology & Marketing*, *33*(7), 486–504.

Dumont, R. G., & Foss, D. C. (1972). *The American view of death: Acceptance or denial?* Cambridge, MA: Schenkman Publishing Company.

Durkin, K. F. (2003). Death, dying and the dead in popular culture. In C. D. Bryant (Ed.), *Handbook of death and dying* (pp. 43–49). London: Sage.

Egginton, W. (2016). Afterword: What are we talking about when we talk about zombies? In J. E. Browning, D. Castillo, D. Schmid & D. A. Reilly (Eds.), *Zombie talk: Culture, history, politics* (pp. 108–114). New York, NY: Palgrave Macmillan.

Fink, M. (2010). AIDS vampires: Reimagining illness in Octavia Butler's "Fledgling". *Science Fiction Studies*, *37*(3), 416–432.

Foltyn, J. L. (2016). Bodies of evidence: Criminalising the celebrity corpse. *Mortality*, *21*(3), 246–262.

Foltyn, J. L. (2008a). The corpse in contemporary culture: Identifying, transacting, and recoding the dead body in the twenty-first century. *Mortality*, *13*(2), 99–104.

Foltyn, J.L. (2008b). Dead famous and dead sexy: Popular culture, forensics, and the rise of the corpse. *Mortality*, *13*(2), 153–173.

Foltyn, J. L. (2008c). Dead sexy: Why death is the new sex. In S. Earle, C. Bartholomew & C. Komaromy (Eds.), *Making sense of death, dying and bereavement: An anthology* (pp. 47–51). Thousand Oaks, CA: Sage.

Foltyn, J. L. (2009). Corpse chic: Dead models and living corpses in fashion photography. *Fashion Forward*, 379–392.

Foltyn, J. L. (2011). Corpse chic: Dead models and living corpses in fashion photography. *Fashion Forward*, 379–92.

Foucault, M. (1973). The birth of the clinic, trans. A. Sheridan, London: Tavistock.

Foucault, M. (1980) The eye of power. In C. Gordon (Ed.), *Power/Knowledge: Selected interviews and other writings 1972–1977* (pp. 146–165). Sussex: Harvester Press.

Francis, L. P. & Francis, J. G. (2010). Stateless crimes, legitimacy, and international criminal law: The case of organ trafficking. *Criminal Law and Philosophy*, 4(3), 283–295.

Freud, S. (1915). Thoughts for the times on war and death. In J. Strachey (Ed.), *The standard edition of the complete psychological works of Sigmund Freud* (Vol. 14, pp. 275–300). London: Hogarth Press.

Frow, J. (1998). Is Elvis a god? Cult, culture, questions of method. *International Journal of Cultural Studies*, 1(2), 197–210.

Furedi, F. (2013). *Moral crusades in an age of mistrust: The Jimmy Savile scandal*. London: Springer.

George, S., &Hughes, B. (2013). Introduction: Undead reflections: the sympathetic vampire and its monstrous other. *Gothic Studies*, 15(1), 1–7.

Gies, L. (2011). Stars behaving badly: Inequality and transgression in celebrity culture. *Feminist Media Studies*, 11(3), 347–361.

Giles, D. (2000). *Illusions of immortality: A psychology of fame and celebrity*. Basingstoke: Palgrave Macmillan.

Giles, D. (2017). The immortalisation of celebrities. In M. H. Jacobsen (Ed.), *Postmortal society: Multidisciplinary perspectives on death, survivalism and immortality in contemporary culture* (pp.97–113). Abingdon-on-Thames: Routledge.

Gorer, G. (1955). The pornography of death. *Encounter*, 5(4), 49–52.

Haddow, G. (2005). The phenomenology of death, embodiment and organ transplantation. *Sociology of Health & Illness*, 27(1), 92–113.

Halbert, D. J. (1999). *Intellectual property in the information age.* London: Quorum Books.

Heinich, N. (1996). *The glory of Van Gogh: An anthropology of admiration*, P. Browne (Trans.), Princeton, NJ: Princeton.

Holmberg, T., Schwennesen, N., & Webster, A. (2011). Bio-objects and the bio-objectification process. *Croatian Medical Journal*, 52(6), 740–742.

Howarth, G. (2016). *Last rites: The work of the modern funeral director.* Abingdon-on-Thames: Routledge.

Hubner, L., Leaning, M., & Manning, P. (Eds.), (2014). *The zombie renaissance in popular culture.* Basingstoke: Palgrave Macmillan.

Illich, I. (1976). *Limits to medicine.* New York, NY: Penguin.

Jones, D. (2002). *Horror: A thematic history in fiction and television.* London: Arnold.

Jones, S., & Jensen, J. (Eds.). (2005). *Afterlife as afterimage: Understanding posthumous fame* (Vol. 2). Bern: Peter Lang.

Jonsson, A. (2015). Post-mortem social death–exploring the absence of the deceased. *Contemporary Social Science*, 10(3), 284–295.

Kayton, L. (1972). The relationship of the vampire legend to schizophrenia. *Journal of Youth and Adolescence*, 1(4), 303–314.

Kearl, M. C. (1995). Death in popular culture. In J. B. Williamson & E. S. Shneidman (Eds.), *Death: Current perspectives* (4th ed., pp. 23–30). New York, NY: McGraw-Hill.

Kearl, M. C. (2010). The proliferation of postselves in American civic and popular cultures. *Mortality*, *15*(1), 47–63.

Kellehear, A. (1984). Are we a 'death-denying' society? A sociological review. *Social Science & Medicine*, *18*(9), 713–721.

Kellehear, A. (2007). *A social history of dying*. Cambridge: Cambridge University Press.

Khapaeva, D. (2017). *The celebration of death in contemporary culture*. Ann Arbor, MI: University of Michigan Press.

Kitch, C., & Hume, J. (2008) *Journalism in a culture of grief*. Abingdon-on-Thames: Routledge.

Kitzinger, C., & Kitzinger, J. (2014) 'This in-between': How families talk about death in relation to severe brain injury and discorders of consciousness. In L. Van Brussel & N. Carpentier (Eds.), *The social construction of death: Interdisciplinary perspectives* (pp. 239–258). Basingstoke: Palgrave Macmillan.

Klaver, E. (2006). *Sites of autopsy in contemporary culture*. New York, NY: State University of New York Press.

Kristeva, J. (1982). *The powers of horror: An essay on abjection*. L. S. Roudiez (Trans.), New York, NY: Columbia University Press.

Lauro, S. J., & Embry, K. (2008). A zombie manifesto: The nonhuman condition in the era of advanced capitalism. *BOUNDARY 2*, *35*(1), 85.

Le Breton, D. (1993). *La chair à vif usages médicaux et mondains du corps humain. [Flesh to the quick: Medical and worldly uses of the human body]*. Paris: Metailie.

Lindenbaum, S., & Lock, M. M. (Eds.). (1993). *Knowledge, power, and practice: The anthropology of medicine and everyday life* (Vol. 36). Los Angeles, CA: University of California Press.

Lipsitz, G. (1990). *Time passages: collective memory and American popular culture*. Minneapolis, MN: University of Minnesota.

Lock, M. (2002). *Twice dead: Organ transplants and the reinvention of death*. Berkeley, CA: University of California Press.

Lofland, L. H. (1979). *The craft of dying: The modern face of death*. London: Sage.

Marcuse, H. (1962). *Eros and civilisation*. New York, NY: Vintage Books.

McCombs, M., & Ghanem, S. I. (2001). The convergence of agenda setting and framing. In S. D. Reese, O. Gandy & A. E. Grant (Eds.), *Framing public life* (pp. 67–81). Abingdon-on-Thames: Routledge.

McCormick, L. (2015). The agency of dead musicians. *Contemporary Social Science, 10*(3), 323–335.

McIlwain, C. D. (2005). *When death goes pop: Death, media and the remaking of community*. New York, NY: Peter Lang.

McKenny, G. P. (1999). The integrity of the body: Critical remarks on a persistent theme in bioethics. In M. J. Cherry (Ed.), *Persons and their bodies: Rights, responsibilities and relationships* (pp. 353–361). Netherlands: Springer.

Midgley, M. (2004). *The myths we live by*. Abingdon-on-Thames: Routledge.

Miller, J. G. (1978). *Living systems*. New York, NY: McGraw-Hill.

Mills, C. W. (1959). *The sociological imagination*. Oxford: Oxford University Press.

Morgan, S. E., Harrison, T. R., Chewning, L., Davis, L. & DiCorcia, M. (2007). Entertainment (Mis)education: The framing of organ donation in entertainment television. *Health Communication*, 22(2), 143–151.

Morgan, S. E., Harrison, T. R., Long S. D., Afifi W. A., Stephenson, M. S., & Reichert, T. (2005). Family discussions about organ donation: how the media influences opinions about donation decisions. *Clinical Transplant*, 19, 674–682.

Morgan, S. E., King, A. J., Smith, J. R., & Ivic, R. (2010). A kernel of truth? The impact of television storylines exploiting myths about organ donation on the public's willingness to donate. *Journal of Communication*, 60(4), 778–796.

Morgan, S. E., Movius, L., & Cody, M. J. (2009). The power of narratives: The effect of entertainment television organ donation storylines on the attitudes, knowledge, and behaviors of donors and nondonors. *Journal of Communication*, 59(1), 135–151.

Morgan, S. E., Palmgreen, P., Stephenson, M., Hoyle, R., & Lorch, E. (2003). Associations between formal message features and subjective evaluations of the sensation value of anti-drug public service announcements. *Journal of Communication*, 53, 1–15.

Mulvey, L. (1989). *Visual and other pleasures*. Basingstoke: Palgrave Macmillan.

Muntean, N., & Payne, M. T. (2009). Attack of the livid dead: Recalibrating terror in the post-September 11 zombie film. In A. Schopp & M. B. Hill (Eds.), *The War on Terror and American popular culture: September 11* (pp. 239–258). Madison, NJ: Fairleigh Dickinson University Press.

Nullis-Kapp, C. (2004). Organ trafficking and transplantation pose new challenges. *Bulletin of the World Health Organization, 82*(9), 715.

O'Neill, R. D. (2006). 'Frankenstein to futurism': Representations of organ donation and transplantation in popular culture. *Transplantation Reviews, 20*, 222–230.

Pearsall, P., Schwartz, G., & Russek, L. (1999). Changes in heart transplant recipients that parallel the personalities of their donors. *Integrative Medicine, 2*(2/3), 65–72.

Penfold-Mounce, R. (2009). *Celebrity culture and crime: The joy of transgression*. Basingstoke: Palgrave Macmillan.

Penfold-Mounce, R. (2010). Consuming criminal corpses: Fascination with the dead criminal body. *Mortality, 15*(3), 250–265.

Penfold-Mounce, R. (2015). Conducting frivolous research in neoliberal universities: what is the value of glossy topics? *Celebrity Studies, 6*(2), 254–257.

Penfold-Mounce, R., Beer, D., & Burrows, R. (2011). *The Wire* as social-science fiction? *Sociology, 45*(1), 152–167.

Pifer, L. (2011). Slacker bites back: Shaun of the Dead finds new life for deadbeats. In D. Christie & J. Lauro (Eds.), *Better off dead: The evolution of the zombie as post human* (pp. 163–174). New York, NY: Fordham University Press.

Pierson, D. P. (2010). Evidential bodies: The forensic and abject gazes in CSI: Crime Scene Investigation. *Journal of Communication Inquiry*, *34*(2), 184–203.

Platts, T. K. (2013). Locating zombies in the sociology of popular culture. *Sociology Compass*, *7*(7), 547–560.

Posel, D., & Gupta, P. (2009) The life of the corpse: Framing reflections and questions. *African Studies*, *68*, 299–309.

Punter, D., & Byron, G. (2004). *The gothic*. London: Wiley.

Reed, D., & Penfold-Mounce, R. (2015). Zombies and the sociological imagination: 'The Walking Dead' as social-science fiction. In L. Hubner, M. Leaning & P. Manning (Eds.), *The zombie renaissance in popular culture* (pp. 124–138). Basingstoke: Palgrave Macmillan.

Reese, S. D. (2001). Prologue - Framing public life: A bridging model for media research. In S. Reese, O. Gandy & A. Grant (Eds.), *Framing public life: Perspectives on media and our understanding of the social world* (pp. 1–27). Abingdon-on-Thames: Routledge.

Rojek, C. (2001). *Celebrity*. Abingdon-on-Thames: John Wiley & Sons, Ltd.

Rugg, J. (2000). Defining the place of burial: what makes a cemetery a cemetery? *Mortality*, *5*(3), 259–275.

Rugg, J. (2006). Lawn cemeteries: the emergence of a new landscape of death. *Urban History*, *33*(2), 213–233.

Russell, J. (2005). *Book of the dead: The complete history of zombie cinema*. Godalming: FAB.

Scheper-Hughes, N. (2001). Commodity fetishism in organs trafficking. *Body & Society*, *7*(31), 31–62.

Schilling, C. (2004). *The body in culture, technology and society*. London: Sage.

Schwartz, G. E., & Russek, L. G. (1997). Dynamical energy systems and modern physics: fostering the science and spirit of complementary and alternative medicine. *Alternative Therapies Healthy Medicine*, *3*(3), 46–56.

Schwartz, G. E., & Russek, L. G. (1998). The origin of holism and memory in nature: the systemic memory hypothesis. *Frontier Perspectives*, *7*(2), 23–30.

Seltzer, M. (1998). *Serial killers: Life and death in America's wound culture*. New York, NY: Routledge.

Sharpley, R., & Stone, P. R. (Eds.). (2009). *The darker side of travel: The theory and practice of dark tourism* (Vol. 41). Bristol: Channel View Publications.

Silver, A. (2010). *Twilight* is not good for maidens: gender, sexuality, and the family in Stephanie Meyer's *Twilight* series. *Studies in the Novel*, *42*(1), 121–138.

Slatman, J., & Widdershoven, G. (2010). Hand transplants and bodily integrity. *Body & Society*, *16*(3), 69–92.

Squier, S. M. (2002). Transplant medicine and transformative narrative, or is science fiction 'rubbish'? In D. Pastourmatzi (Ed.), *Biotechnological and medical themes in science fiction* (pp. 87–110). Thessaloniki: University Studio Press.

Stone, P., & Sharpley, R. (2008). Consuming dark tourism: A thanatological perspective. *Annals of Tourism Research*, *35*(2), 574–595.

Penfold-Mounce, R. (2015). Conducting frivolous research in neoliberal universities: what is the value of glossy topics? *Celebrity Studies*, *6*(2), 254–257.

Sugg, R. (2011). *Mummies, cannibals and vampires: The history of corpse medicine from the Renaissance to the Victorians*. Abingdon-on-Thames: Routledge.

Sylvia, C. (1997). *A change of heart: A memoir*, New York, NY: Warner Books.

Tenga, A., & Zimmerman, E. (2013). Vampire gentlemen and zombie beasts: A rendering of true monstrosity. *Gothic Studies*, *15*(1), 76–87.

Thornton, J. I., & Peterson, J. L. (2002). The general assumptions and rationale of forensic identification. In D. L. Faigman, D. H. Kaye, M. J. Saks & J. Sanders (Eds.), *Science in the law: Forensic science issues* (pp. 1–45). Eagan, MN: West.

Timmermans, S. (2006). *Postmortem: How medical examiners explain suspicious deaths*. Chicago, IL: University of Chicago Press.

Turner, B. (1984). *The body and society*. Oxford: Blackwell.

van Riper, A. B. (2003). What the public thinks it knows about science. Popular culture and its role in shaping the public's perception of science and scientists. *EMBO Rep*, *4*(12), 1104–1107.

Vincent, R. (2015). *Vampires as a tool to destabilize contemporary notions of gender and sexuality. Undergraduate Prizes and Awards*. Paper 17, University of New Orleans. Retrieved from http://scholarworks.uno.edu/awards/17.

Walter, T. (1991). Modern death: taboo or not taboo? *Sociology*, *25*(2), 293–310.

Walter, T. (2009). Jade's dying body: The ultimate reality show. *Sociological Research Online*, 14(5).

Walters, G. D. (2004). Understanding the popular appeal of horror cinema: An integrated-interactive model. *Journal of Media Psychology*, *9*(2), 1–35.

Weber, T. (2014). Representation of corpses in contemporary television. In L. Van Brussel & N. Carpentier (Eds.), *The social construction of death: Interdisciplinary perspectives* (pp. 75–91). Basingstoke: Palgrave Macmillan.

Weed, C. M. (2009). *The zombie manifesto: The Marxist revolutions in George A. Romero's 'Land of the Dead'*. Waco, TX: Baylor University.

Weisman, A. D. (1972). *On dying and denying: A psychiatric study of terminality*. New York, NY: Behavioural Publications.

Williamson, M. (2005). *The lure of the vampire: Gender, fiction and fandom from Bram Stoker to Buffy*. New York, NY: Wallflower Press.

Woodthorpe, K. (2010). Public dying: Death in the media and Jade Goody. *Sociology Compass*, *4*(5), 283–294.

Woodthorpe, K. (2011a). Using bereavement theory to understand memorialising behaviour. *Bereavement Care*, *30*(2), 29–32.

Woodthorpe, K. (2011b). Sustaining the contemporary cemetery: Implementing policy alongside conflicting perspectives and purpose. *Mortality*, *16*(3), 259–276.

Youngner, S. J. (1996). Some must die. In S. J. Youngner, R. C. Fox & L. J. O'Connell (Eds.), *Organ transplantation: Meanings and realities* (pp. 32–55). Madison, WI: University of Wisconsin.

Zilboorg, G. (1943). Fear of death. *The psychoanalytic quarterly*, *12*, 465–475.

Zimmermann, C., & Rodin, G. (2004). The denial of death thesis: sociological critique and implications for palliative care. *Palliative Medicine*, *18*(2), 121–128.

INDEX